WATCH OUT FOR PIRATES

TALES FROM A TRAVEL WRITER'S LIFE

JULES BROWN

TRUST-ME TRAVEL

PRAISE FOR JULES BROWN'S BOOKS

'The best kind of travel companion – funny, informed and always up for an adventure.'

MARTIN DUNFORD, ROUGH GUIDES FOUNDER

'I laughed out aloud so much that I scared the cat!'

AMAZON REVIEWER (5 STARS)

'This is the kind of travel writing I love – full of charming moments, unusual sights and a writer who is determined to discover what really makes a place unique.'

AMAZON REVIEWER (5 STARS)

'A very funny travel writer ... I highly recommend this journey.'

EDIE JAROLIM, AUTHOR OF GETTING NAKED FOR MONEY

'Brown is not only a great traveller, he's a brilliant story-teller ... This is travel writing at its best.'

HEIDI SLOWINSKI, US BOOK REVIEWER

'I feel I have been travelling ... with a new, entertainingly witty friend.'

SUE BAVEY, UK BOOK REVIEWER

'I highly recommend it if you are looking for a quick, fun, travel-fuelled read.'

'What captivated me from the start was the author's style of writing and sense of humour.'

'Superb, touching, fun and informative. Jules is a wonderful writer and his conversational style and sharp observations are a joy to read.'

'I loved it, I'm hooked and will read more of Jules' work. Can I carry your rucksack next time?'

'For me this is a perfect travel book. The visual writing sweeps you along with Jules as he explores offbeat places and events.'

'His style of writing is informative whilst remaining chatty and intimate, like having a friend telling you of their travel adventures. Jules writes with his heart and soul.'

CONTENTS

PART ONE
WATCH OUT FOR PIRATES

Introduction	3
Good morning, Bangkok	5
Tipping for beginners in New York	17
Crikey! Driving across outback Australia	28
Wasting time and money in Yorkshire	42
Permission to land in Luxor	54
Capital punishment in Montenegro	63
Serving up groundnut soup in Ghana	72
Behind the scenes in Blackpool	81
A wedding crasher in Sicily	91
On the Outlander trail in Scotland	101
Living the dream in Portugal	114
Watch out for pirates	127

PART TWO
BONUS CHAPTERS

Travel + writer: an insider's guide	141
Six things you should never leave home without	144
Finding a room at the end of the world	153
Tourist or traveller?	163
Awesome hidden gems in a land of contrasts	167
Why you don't really need a guidebook	179

Also by Jules Brown   193
Did you like this book?   195
About the author   197
Find out more   199

PART ONE
WATCH OUT FOR PIRATES

INTRODUCTION

A review of one of my books once said that travel writer is up there with panda cuddler and wine taster as far as dream jobs go. I get that a lot, and obviously it would be churlish to say that the job is not like that at all – no one wants to hear a travel writer moaning on about how hard it is to visit exotic places, stay in lovely hotels and eat nice dinners.

So you won't find me complaining about any of it, even when things go a bit wrong, as they often do. In this book alone, there are stories about visiting Bangkok, New York, Australia, Egypt, Ghana, Sicily, Montenegro, Portugal and Scotland. I drive across the outback, walk the rugged English coast, float in a balloon over Luxor, and cruise up and down the Chao Phraya River.

I can't lie, I've had a fine old time as a travel writer, and if you've read my other travel memoirs – *Don't Eat the Puffin* and *Never Pack an Ice-Axe* – you'll know that it's often the journey, as much as the destination, that's at the heart of every story. There's a crazy cast of characters in this book too, from irate waiters to Highland warriors, and you'll meet my one-of-a-kind Dad again, whose influence had a lot to do with my travel-writing career. This time, you'll also meet *his* Dad, my grandfather, which is where the pirates come in, and at the end of it all – despite the spills and scrapes – you'll still probably think that being a travel writer is not a bad old life.

And yet.

Like any job, there are bits of being a travel writer that don't make it into the stories. In the same way that you don't see all the bamboo-sorting that has to take place before pandas are cuddled, I tend not to include the day-to-day aspects of the job. But you might find them interesting nonetheless, which is why I've thrown in some bonus chapters about what it's like to be a travel guide-book writer, which is the gig I did for Rough Guides for over thirty years. Let's just say that there's often another story behind those straightforward bits of advice – packing tips, finding a room, seeing the sights – that you read in every guide.

Then, the next time you pick up a travel book, maybe – just maybe – you'll spare a thought for those with the toughest of jobs. No, not travel writer. Did you know a panda will rip your face off, soon as look at you, especially if you try and force a glass of wine down its throat?

GOOD MORNING, BANGKOK

TRAVEL WRITERS DON'T TALK MUCH about being frightened. We're supposed to be intrepid adventurers, alive to new experiences, although I draw the line at jumping out of things or off things. And travel writers definitely aren't supposed to be frightened of travel itself. Going to foreign parts is what we do. We seek out the new and different. We boldly go. And I have boldly gone to places all over the world, only there's a first time for everything and I'm the sort of inherently anxious person that always over-thinks and catastrophises.

Don't look where you don't want to go, is what they say. Well, I invariably have a good old look as far into the potentially catastrophic future as possible. I'm famous for it.

Which is why I was standing inside Bangkok airport one morning in front of the exit doors, watching them swoosh open and then close again as arriving passengers churned past me and disappeared into the bright light beyond.

Everyone else was going "Woohoo, Bangkok!" or "Hello mum" and piling out of the airport into the city. Meanwhile, I was loitering in the air-conditioned arrivals hall, surrounded by familiar signs and fast-food outlets, looking out of the intermittently open doors into a vast sea of broiled humanity and going – "No, you're all right, thanks, I'll just wait here a bit longer. Maybe get a Big Mac."

I was frightened. Well, perhaps more anxious than frightened, but it amounted to the same thing after a tension-building, two-day journey to get here on my first visit to Southeast Asia. Two days, incidentally, because my connecting flight from the UK had been late, which meant an enforced stopover for the night in the Gulf state of Bahrain. There had been plane-wide groans at that, but not from me, which was how anxious I was about flying into Thailand for the first time. A twenty-four-hour delay in an airline-approved, chain hotel with cable TV, where all meals are provided and you can't really leave your squeaky clean room in between times? Yes, excellent, if that meant delaying the inevitable arrival, make it a week.

And what was I anxious or frightened about? That's the thing. Nothing really. What exactly was the problem here? Thailand was just a new country. I'd been to new countries before. I was a travel writer. I knew how to do this stuff. You just show your passport and in you go.

But there's a first time for everything, and Southeast

Asia was a big jump for someone who had only travelled around Europe thus far. I didn't think knowledge of the Lisbon tram system or the ability to order from an Italian menu was going to help me much.

Obviously, I'd been to places before where I didn't understand the local population, however slowly they spoke – Scotland, for example. But Thailand seemed to be of a different order altogether. There was no getting away from it, I was nervous – about not understanding people, not being understood, not being able to read Thai, getting lost, offending people by mistake, eating bits of animals I didn't really want to eat, getting sick and being robbed. I was also quite concerned about squat toilets and spiders.

None of these things, individually, was a genuine fear (toilets *plus* spiders, now that was a genuine fear), but they all added up to an extreme feeling of nervousness for an anxious person about to land on a new continent.

They were also all ridiculous, let's be clear about that. I'm a white, middle-class man from Western Europe and all those concerns of mine played right to the racist tropes and attitudes that people often have towards many countries in the developing world. Thailand, funny food and dodgy toilets, and no one speaks English, how on earth will I cope?

It's easy to look back, thirty years later, and under-stand how my cultural conditioning underpinned my natural anxiety about new things and places. All I can say is that, at the time, while I really wanted to visit Thailand, the prospect of setting foot outside the airport door was making me very nervous indeed. I knew it would be fine – probably – but I had a sinking feeling in the pit of my stomach and a racing heart, and I couldn't do anything about it except step off the edge and hope for the best.

I could have gone home again, I suppose – and there were full minutes when that seemed like an excellent idea – but when I imagined the shame, the epaulettes being torn off my travel-writer uniform, the sword being broken across the knee, I got a grip and confronted Southeast Asia.

The guidebooks can't prepare you for the reality of the first few minutes in a completely new environment. One day, I imagine that the *Rough Guide to the Moon* will talk matter-of-factly about the short walk from the airlock to the lunar reception building, but behind those few words will hide the click and hiss of the closing door, the sound of your breath in the helmet and the crunch of moondust beneath your feet. I had a *Lonely Planet Thailand* guide which told me that I could save some money by ignoring the air-con shuttle service and catching a local bus into the city from outside the airport. That sounded entirely normal and do-able.

Maybe now, with YouTube, TikTok, Instagram and Anthony Bourdain TV programmes, first-time visitors anywhere are more prepared for what things will be like. Back then, I just had a couple of mundane sentences in a book to go on, and no real idea what was outside the sanctuary of the airport.

There was a whoosh from the closing door behind me and then – basically, bedlam. Even at the airport, where presumably there was some kind of order and method in place otherwise the planes would never take off, Bangkok seemed like one enormous melee. Quite apart from the disgorged passengers and their towering luggage trolleys, there were people hauling candy-striped bags the size of small houses and others carrying huge water bottles you could bathe a baby elephant in. If there was a taxi rank and an orderly queue, I couldn't see it, but there were about a million taxi drivers shouting at anyone who emerged from the scrum. Behind them was a second wave of *tuk-tuks*, bicycles, scooters and possibly unicycles, all weaving in and out of a crowd of people who sounded like they had just been ejected from a stadium for shouting too loudly.

Again, I know. Shouty, loud, foreign people was my default understanding of the situation. In my defence, the scene and the noise were unlike anything I had ever encountered before, and when you added in the blast of muggy heat that instantly turned my back sopping wet under my rucksack, it was some welcome to Thailand. Was that heat even normal? Possibly I was having a heart attack, in which case that would be fine, I'd surely be carried back inside the nice, cool airport? Please let it be a heart attack.

It wasn't. It was Bangkok.

Somehow, I found the right bus, going in the right direction, and squeezed in with my pack. The bus driver took some money out of my palm – could have been cents, could have been a week's wages – and I jammed myself in by a window. The traffic outside was insane – it was impossible to tell which side of the road was which, because vehicles were just weaving their way through every available space. The heat inside the bus was even worse than outside. I had a guidebook map, hopelessly out of scale, which I tried to follow, but it was hard to spot landmarks from a city bus caught bumper-to-bumper in a dozen lanes of snarling traffic.

I'd also never been on such a crowded bus before, with people crushed right against me as I straddled my backpack, clinging on to it with my knees in case one of those thieves I was concerned about tried to make off with it – though good luck to anyone who actually wanted to get off the bus at any point.

When it did stop, half the bus had to empty out to allow a single person off, at which point everyone piled on again, along with any new passengers caught up in the maelstrom. You could have just been walking along the street minding your own business, and chances are you'd suddenly find yourself on the bus, whether you wanted to be or not. There were probably people on the bus who had stepped out of their front door that morning to have a cigarette or pick up the post and now found themselves twenty miles away in the Greater Bangkok area in their slippers. There were probably people who had been been born on that bus and never yet managed to get off.

However, after a while spent pressed very tightly against various strangers, an interesting thing happened to my body. No, not that, what are you like? Actually, I calmed down. My stomach and heart stopped sinking and racing. I began to take in my surroundings. Everything was very strange and very different, but it seemed that this was just a bus and these were all just people going about their daily lives. Could it be that there was nothing much to worry about? Other than the fact that it would have been quicker to walk from airport to city centre, so slow was our progress.

I didn't learn a lesson on that bus – nothing so trite – but I did start to breathe more easily. A bit like on the plane over, I was perfectly happy if the journey went on quite a while longer, now that I was in some sort of protected zone. I didn't understand much of what was going on outside – from the roadside signs to the food sold by street vendors, it was all a bit of a mystery – but I appreciated my window view as we trundled inexorably towards the city. In the end, after a bit more fruitless worrying about where exactly we were, I simply got off the bus when everyone else did, at the end of the line.

If the bus had been crowded, the city streets were even more packed, and I was buffeted this way and that as I stood there plotting my next move. It was ferociously hot and humid, I was wearing all the wrong clothes, and the sun was already scalding my neck. At least, I assumed it was the sun, because I certainly couldn't see it. Despite the evidence of the intense heat, the sky was a sort of washed-out grey that melded into a general haze the further into the distance I looked. Or perhaps my eyeballs had just melted.

The city smell, too, was new to me – a kind of sour-sweetness that was at least one part traffic fumes, one part rubbish truck, one part open gutter, and one part market stall selling over-ripe fruit. Maybe even some incense in there too. When I breathed in, the scent filled my entire head; it was more a taste than a smell. It was ever-present wherever I went for the next two weeks, and yet I pretty much stopped noticing it after a day or two. I can smell it now though, sitting at my desk thirty years later, with my eyes closed, just before writing these words.

I was less anxious by now. Bangkok seemed possible, even if I was overwhelmed by the noise, heat and smell. For starters, I'd spent some local currency, got on and off a bus, and had stood on a Thai pavement. Those were distinct achievements. It was all going swimmingly. And the truth about my travel anxiety in those early days was that, ultimately, I never let it put me off. I wanted to see new places more than I was frightened of going to new places, so I always just stepped off the edge and hoped for the best.

Because of this in-built determination – one of the things, I suppose, that made me a travel writer – I'd caught a local, public bus, rather than take the tourist shuttle or a taxi from the airport. That seemed like an important thing to do, right at the outset – experience the real Bangkok. And it's why I then followed a sketchy guidebook map through crowded, narrow alleys, down to the river.

Nearly all foreign backpackers stayed in a travellers' enclave called Khaosan Road, where you could buy knock-off designer T-shirts, eat banana pancakes, and listen to Bob Marley in the company of people just like yourself. However, I thought I could probably do better than that and had found a family-run guesthouse in a different neighbourhood – though as I had found it in the same *Lonely Planet* guide that was sending people to Khaosan Road, on reflection it was no more 'real' or 'authentic', or any of the other terribly misguided things that I thought at the time.

Still, it did mean dealing with more of Bangkok before I could rest up with a beer and a banana pancake, which in turn meant finding my way to the Chao Phraya River, which winds through the centre of the city. Ironically, given that I'd already mastered the local bus service, I was following good guidebook advice, which was that the best way of getting around the city was not by overcrowded bus but by river boat.

I shouldered my pack and shuffled down covered alleys towards the river, looking for a boat pier. It was part market, part thoroughfare, and again, I'd quickly get used to the scene, but on that first day it felt like I'd been dumped back several centuries. This was not what markets were like where I came from. I couldn't see a pork pie or a pick 'n' mix stall anywhere.

An open drain ran down the centre of the alley, crossed here and there by boards, and the stalls tightly flanked both sides so that you brushed against piled produce as you passed by. Only some of it was familiar; largely, it seemed that unless it was knobbly, hairy or of a hitherto unknown colour, it didn't really count as a fruit or vegetable. Most people wore plastic flip-flops on their feet, and the traders were in shorts and singlets, all of which were far more sensible than the sweaty clothes and footwear I had on. Though to be fair, mine weren't covered in animal blood or entrails.

At a line of stalls, fish – chopped in half across the middle – were suspended on hooks and if they were no longer exactly alive, then they weren't quite dead yet either. Their mouths opened and closed at eye level as I inched past. It's tough to look a fish in the eye at the best of times, and these were not the best of times for the fish. If you'd asked me five minutes earlier, "Would you like to walk down a dark alley with zombie fish, where men with bloody cleavers smile at you?", I may have thought sod it and headed for Khaosan Road instead, but by now I was committed. There wasn't anywhere to turn round, in any case. I certainly wasn't going to run the risk of knocking over a pile of furry fruit or having half a fish whisper in my ear.

Miraculously, the boat pier was where the book said it would be, and there was even a pier name in English, so I could figure out which way to go. Over the next few days, the river boats would become my only mode of transport – I never took another bus – because here was a system I could understand. Upriver or down river, get off, look around, then go back again. This way, I saw all of Bangkok that I wanted to see, and if I couldn't reach it by river boat and walking, then I didn't bother.

I got off at the pier indicated in the guidebook and found my way to the comfortingly named Little Home Guest House, which – surprise, surprise – turned out to be in another small enclave of travellers' accommodation. I'm sure everyone staying there thought they'd done something daring and different by avoiding Khaosan Road, but it did feel like an achievement at the time – finding my way there, right across the city, without a word of Thai or any understanding of the culture, and beset by a woeful litany of entirely misguided fears.

I've looked for the Little Home several times over the years, because that's the sort of thing you can do now there's the internet. I'm pretty sure it no longer exists, but the reason I was keen to keep tabs on it is because, when I walked inside that day, on the noticeboard behind the reception desk they had pinned up the airmail letter I had sent them several weeks previously, requesting a room. Told you I was determined. Also ridiculously organised, over-anxious and fretful about arriving in a place without a hotel reservation.

Maybe I did learn a lesson that day. I didn't think about it at the time, because I was too busy checking the toilet situation (not as bad as you'd think, but still fairly bad), inspecting the mysterious net over the bed (what do you mean, mosquitos?) and wondering how big Thai spiders might be. They're massive, by the way.

But those lovely people in the Little Home – normal, regular people, with normal, regular lives in a normal, regular city – couldn't have been more welcoming to a sweaty Englishman so anxious that he'd written them an airmail letter. They'd pinned it up, and not so they could make fun of me when I had arrived, even though that's what I clearly deserved.

They knew my name, had saved me a room, and then poured me a beer in their shaded courtyard, while they took care of the paperwork and made the bed. And later they served me dinner, and poured more beers, and told me the best things to see and do in Bangkok, some of them not involving dark alleys, decapitated fish, and men with cleavers.

We all get anxious or frightened, even travel writers. There are things that will challenge us, wherever we go and whatever we do. But if you're going to get anxious, at least make it about a genuine fear – jumping out of a plane, say, obviously mad – and not an in-built cultural reaction or a lazy stereotype. All I really did that day was catch a bus, walk through a market and check into a hotel – it's just that I did those things six thousand miles away from where I usually did them, in a very hot city wearing entirely inappropriate clothing. Nothing to worry about and all my fault, respectively.

Bangkok was the first place I ever went that truly overwhelmed me. But you know what? It affected me for about a day, because I foolishly let it, and then I bought some flip-flops in the scary market and started to see what Southeast Asia was all about.

TIPPING FOR BEGINNERS IN NEW YORK

THERE's plenty that's terrifying about New York to a first-time visitor.

The subway? You like crazy people? Sure, take the train – maybe check you've got all your limbs when you get off.

You want to what? Walk across downtown? Like, with your legs? Driving, that's a much better idea. Just don't go over fifty, don't take any highway exit marked 'Crack-town' and don't reach into the glove compartment for your licence if you're stopped by the police. Because, you know, guns. What? Oh sure, guns. You'll need a gun, everyone has one.

Taxis? Licensed thrill-rides with amiable psychopaths. Greyhound bus across America? Even the most piratical, thick-set, overly tattooed taxi driver will refuse to take you to the Port Authority Bus Terminal because – unlike their horn-happy, multi-lane driving – "it's not safe."

Sandwich shops and delis? High-pressure decisions

about things you've never heard of – Reuben, hero, Kaiser roll, knish – while crazy people in a line behind you shout, "Move it, bud, this ain't no retirement home."

Coffee shops? Where to start. Like being expected to know how many ounces of *cappuccino* you want isn't enough – ounces, really? – you're then going to be asked whether you want your frothy coffee "Wet or dry?" I mean, they're just trolling the tourists, surely?

It's not like you haven't done your homework. You've tried to prepare. You've watched *Friends* and Woody Allen films, and *When Harry Met Sally*, and imagine that it's going to be quite straightforward. (Don't watch *Taxi Driver*, that won't help at all.) There appears to be lots of sitting around in cafés and diners, zinging one-liners at each other and ordering eggs over easy; that's not too difficult, even if you're not entirely sure what kind of egg that's going to get you. 'Wholewheat toast', by the way? They mean 'brown.'

You know not to ask for the 'toilet', because even New Yorkers will recoil in horror at that uncouth word, and you make yourself say 'bathroom' or 'restroom' instead through gritted teeth, because you don't want a bath or a rest, you want a wee. If you're on the advanced course, you've seen all nine series of *Seinfeld*, which bring you somewhat closer to an understanding of the nuances of daily life in New York.

But it's still not enough. There's worse to come, and it starts the very first time you have to tip someone.

Look, we're not idiots, we're just foreign. We understand how the service economy works; we get the concept of tipping. It's ten percent in a British restaurant. That's about all you need to know. Maybe the same to a taxi driver, if they haven't spent the entire journey being overtly offensive. Sure, the same to the hairdresser if you like. But that really is it. If a posh restaurant expects more than ten percent, they'll add it on to the bill in any case – you don't need to worry about working it out. And as a rule, outside restaurants, you certainly don't need to give tipping a second thought.

But oh, good grief, the stress and anxiety the minute you set foot in New York as a foreign visitor, because you unwisely read the 'etiquette' section in the guidebook on the flight over. You can't even get out of the airport unscathed. It's a dollar a bag for anyone who interacts with your luggage from the minute you step off the plane. Between the skycap, the taxi driver and the bellhop (and bear in mind British people don't know what two of those things are), you could be down twenty bucks by the time you've closed your room door. And there's no chance a Brit is ordering hotel room service, I can tell you that – the fear that that might bring up another fleet of people who all need tipping is too much to bear.

A dollar a bag is at least an understandable amount, I suppose. We can all get on board with that, while pondering the excruciating embarrassment of trying to press a pound coin into the landlady's hand next time we visit an English B&B. They'd think you were either insulting them or propositioning them, and neither is really the way you want to go at Mrs Miggins' Bella Vista Guest House.

It's also a dollar in the bar, every time you have a drink. Now that's a trickier concept for British people. You don't tip in a pub, or at least not in any kind of formal, established way. You could live your whole life in Britain and never leave a tip in a pub and no one would think you were a bad person.

Of course, you *can* tip in a pub – leave the bar-person the change, for example, or ask if they'd like a drink on you. Or say, as one of my oldest friends does, after giving his drinks order, "and your own," which always sounds to me dangerously like a personal slur – imagine it uttered in a thick Lancastrian accent – but which the bar staff of Greater Manchester seem to recognise not as an "Up yours, mate" but a polite invitation to add a pound or two to the bill.

In the States, though, even though *you've* walked up to the bar and all the person has done is pour you a drink – literally their job – you have to tip them. And if you don't, you run the risk of a tongue-lashing, as happened to another friend of mine in New York, whose failure, on his first visit, to leave a dollar bill on the counter resulted in an apoplectic bar-tender chasing him back to his table to call him "Scum." Not, "I'm terribly sorry, but it's customary to tip bartenders in New York," but "Scum."

So, you can see why this is all very concerning. In Britain, you don't have to leave a tip in a bar and in New York it's just another damn thing to remember if you don't want to offend anyone and be shouted at. And as British people, we really don't want to offend anyone, at least not on a personal level. We might in the past have invaded your country, oppressed your citizens and burned down your White House, but water under the bridge and all that. I mean, we're not planning on saying sorry for those things, but equally, we don't want to appear rude with the tipping. It's just, we're not sure of all the rules.

All we really know, because we read the guidebook and watched *Seinfeld*, is that we don't want to under-tip and be chased down the street by an irate waiter. That would be the final straw in a stressful city where we've already eaten a knish and had a wet coffee by mistake. The chasing down the street is not how we want to remember our New York trip. Nobody wants to be George Costanza.

And on the face of it, it's not too hard to avoid. "Just tip fifteen percent," says everyone.

Fifteen is not ten though. Do the maths, it really isn't. It's harder to work out under pressure. It requires the British person to undertake another calculation stage, all the while worrying that they haven't left quite enough to stave off street-chasing. You find yourself rounding up, where in Britain you'd round down; you over-compensate because you really don't want to be yelled at. You pay fifteen percent and more for indifferent, poor and frankly atrocious service because at the end of the day you don't want to exit, pursued by a waiter.

Which is why on my first trip to New York, after a truly terrible Mexican meal in a freezing cold restaurant, where the staff got the order wrong on multiple occasions, I still performed high-level mathematical calculations, possibly on a blackboard, left a weighty tip where none really was required, and thanked everyone profusely on the way out. Wallet lightened considerably but no chasing – the mark of a good night out in the Big Apple.

If only fifteen percent was all there was to worry about. The fancier the restaurant, the higher the service element and, presumably, the faster the waiters. I should think in a Michelin three-star place they can run like Olympic sprinters. As evidence, I present my experience many years ago at the Tribeca Grill, a famed and rather fabulous joint owned by Robert de Niro. It's a beautiful place, in an old coffee warehouse that shows off exposed brickwork and stained-glass chandeliers. You can picture the kind of thing, I'm sure. Let's just say the soup is sixteen dollars and leave it at that.

I was with my New York friends Alan and Cheryl, and baby Lachlan, because that's the kind of thing New Yorkers do – take a baby to Robert de Niro's classy, celeb-filled restaurant, like that's normal. Cheryl took Lachlan to the bathroom – in this instance, who knows, the baby probably needed an actual bath – and was gone an inordinate length of time. Alan and I were smoking cheroots and having a massage by the time she returned, it had been so long. By way of explanation, Cheryl revealed that she had been chatting with a lovely woman in the queue who had made a fuss of Lachlan. Had a cuddle with the baby and everything. Her husband liked babies too, apparently; they were here on a date night.

"That's her, over there," said Cheryl, pointing at a distant table.

So Alan and I waved at Linda McCartney, and at

Paul, sitting next to her, and said "What, you mean Linda and Paul McCartney?" and Cheryl said, "Oh, really?"

That's the kind of place the Tribeca Grill is, and it came as no surprise that the suggested service charge weighed in at twenty percent. That's a full double the normal rate for a British person and therefore the cause of major palpitations. And because of the loveliness of the staff, the excellence of the meal and a side order of McCartney, we nudged it up to twenty-five percent – and twenty-five percent of several hundred dollars is a lot of money to leave as a tip. It would be cheaper just to call in, hand over fifty bucks and not eat anything. As it was, to even things up I felt compelled to steal a copy of the menu, which featured a hand-drawn picture of the restaurant exterior by your actual Robert de Niro. Come on, they must expect that, it's priced in surely – look, not sorry, the pan-fried brussels sprouts are ten dollars. But still, the evening ended without being chased down the street by waiters, and that's the important thing.

That event happened when it was least expected – when I had already been to New York a few times, taken the subway without being murdered, had a pastrami sandwich or two, and generally worked out how not to be permanently alarmed by the city. I was OK with the tipping by this point. Sure, a waiter got sixteen or seventeen percent now and again because I always erred on the side of caution but, on the whole, the prospect of being shouted at by an underemployed actor in a tight-fitting, black T-shirt had receded enough into the distance for me not to be overly concerned by it any more.

Then I got roped in by my publisher to help launch Rough Guides as a travel guidebook series in America. I say 'roped in.' I mean 'flown to New York, put up in a midtown hotel and asked to drink white wine with travel writers.' I did the launching rather well, I thought. I ate canapés and chatted to editors, and drank simply enormous amounts of white wine, because it would have been rude not to. I sat behind a huge pile of *Rough Guide* travel books and gave them away for free, and I signed many, many copies of those books that night – again, it would have been rude not to. If you can find an unsigned copy of a *Rough Guide* today in a second-hand bookstore in New York, you're sitting on gold, I tell you.

After the party, dinner in a nearby restaurant was hosted by the publisher. A dozen of us – travel writers, editors, publishing people – sat around a large table and carried on eating and drinking, racking up a bill that I had no financial interest in. This, by the way, is a travel writer's dream scenario, the sort of thing you hear about at your father's knee – tell me again, Daddy, about the free sirloin and Barolo – but don't dare believe to be true. And not only was the bill being taken care of by someone else, but so – by extension – was the tip. Worry not, was the unspoken message; waiter, another bottle over here.

The final bill must have been enormous. I don't know, I never saw it. The only person who had anything to do with the bill was the host, a British travel publisher, who flourished a credit card and signed the check while the rest of us drained the dregs of whatever was left on the table.

Looking back now, the first sign of trouble was the return of the waiter, who brought the card back and asked if everything had been all right with the meal. Yes, lovely, thanks very much, we all said. Charming staff, very solicitous, we all agreed.

Next up – as we all shuffled around at the table, looking for bags and coats – was the maître d'.

"Excuse me Sir, have you enjoyed your meal this evening?" he asked our host. "Was there anything else we could have done?"

"It's been lovely, thank you," said our host. "Very nice, really."

"It's just," said the maître d', "that there appears to be a problem with the tip."

Problem with the tip. The words somehow rose above the restaurant hubbub and percolated the consciousness of every British person around the table. Primal fear, fight or flight, hackles up, this was it.

"I'm sure that's a mistake," said our host, pointing at the bill and credit card receipt. "I have left a tip, there, you can see."

"Yes," said the maître d', hesitantly, "it's just that you have only left ten percent. Was there something wrong with the meal or the service?"

We all looked down at our shoes or found something fascinating in one of our pockets, while honed in on the increasingly excruciating conversation. The only person who wasn't fazed in the slightest was our host, who came back with the reply, "No, everything was great, thank you. That's the normal tip, ten percent."

Really, where to start with this? The man was a travel publisher, with a guidebook series that included books about New York and America. He only had to read one of his own books to know that this was fighting talk.

To be fair to the maître d', he heard the majority accent around the table and tried to cut our host some slack.

"Sir, if I may, usually if you've enjoyed your meal, fifteen to twenty percent service would be considered normal."

By now, it goes without saying, you could hear a pin drop in the restaurant. No one had thought they were getting a floor show with their rib-eye; this was turning out to be one of the most entertaining nights many diners had had in a long while.

Our man was undeterred. Wrong but undeterred. "Well, ten percent seems like a reasonable tip to me. I always tip ten percent."

The maître d' had had enough, you could tell. "And what, Sir" – and that Sir had disdain stitched right through it – "do they say, when you tip ten percent?"

Fair play to the maître d', he thought his case was unanswerable, but then again, he didn't realise he was dealing with someone who was British and therefore couldn't imagine that he was in any way wrong or mistaken.

"They say, 'thank you very much'."

It was a good reply, if I'm honest. Not the table-turning retort our host imagined, but still a valiant attempt at regaining the moral high ground. There were no winners here, though.

We all got to our feet in a silent restaurant and filed out under the resentful gaze of waiters, diners, kitchen staff and passers-by at the window, curious to see how this would play out. No one said a word about to it our host, who didn't think he'd done anything wrong in any case, and we all trooped off down the street, utterly mortified and awaiting the sound of an angry waiter's pounding feet. None came, probably on the agreed basis back in the restaurant that the public shaming had been sufficient.

So ever since then, when people have asked me for recommendations in New York, I only have one piece of advice for them.

Practice working out ten percent of an amount; half it and add that to the amount; round that up to the nearest dollar and add a bit more; have a think about it and add a bit more still; and then, when you get up to leave the restaurant table, throw down another dollar or two, just in case. If it keeps you awake that night, you can always go back the next day and slip the waiter another ten-spot. Basically, anything to avoid the culturally loaded question, "Has everything been all right with the meal?"

If you hear that phrase, reach for your wallet or hope you've got your running shoes on.

CRIKEY! DRIVING ACROSS OUTBACK AUSTRALIA

You want to know what gives you a jolt first thing in the morning? Better than a double-shot espresso?

Coming round the front of your vehicle to find a three-foot-long monitor lizard standing guard in the sun.

"Go on then," she said.

"I don't think so."

"What are you frightened of?"

"That. Obviously."

"It's just a lizard," she said.

"It's massive and it's got claws."

"Well, you'll have to do something, we need to get in the van," she said, which was true but not helpful.

I took another look. I'd seen lizards before, on rocks in the Mediterranean; they were about four inches long and disappeared at the first sound of footsteps. This giant specimen looked like it had eaten all those lizards in the Mediterranean and it was going nowhere. Godzilla was currently standing between us and a two-thousand-mile

28

drive across the Red Centre of Australia in a rented campervan.

"What would Steve Irwin do?" she said, which was an excellent question.

Steve Irwin – a larger-than-life Australian wildlife expert known as 'The Crocodile Hunter' – was one of the very reasons we were about to embark on this trip. We liked Steve and his TV programmes. There wasn't a scaled, fanged, razor-toothed, clawed, deadly or venomous animal that Steve wouldn't tackle, armed only with a tight pair of khaki shorts and the indiscriminate use of the word 'Crikey'. He and his family had a wildlife park outside Brisbane, which was to be the end-point – nay, highlight – of our trip.

Yet here we were in Alice Springs, half a continent away, stymied by a big lizard.

"Steve would wrestle it to the ground. I'm not doing that."

"It's more afraid of you, than you are of it."

"I'm not falling for that again. You said that about the wallaby. It wasn't the slightest bit afraid. It chased me."

"It hopped near you a bit."

"Hop, chase, I didn't notice you helping."

In the end, it turned out that the way to get a Sand Monitor to move is to flap about a bit in front of it while someone else toots a horn and revs the engine. Eventually, it got the message and sloped off, leaving the road clear.

Lizards aside, the route from Alice Springs to Brisbane is fairly straightforward, on account of there not being many roads to confuse matters in the middle of Australia. Drive three hundred miles north along the Stuart Highway in the Northern Territory and turn right just about covers it, after which there are only another couple of turns all the way to Queensland and Brisbane. You barely need a map.

There is one early call to make, about forty miles north of Alice, where Route 12 – the so-called Plenty Highway – cuts east across the outback towards Queensland. Go this way and you'd save three hundred miles of driving, but if you're in a rental vehicle and don't know what you're doing, you really shouldn't do that. It's a dirt road with "long stretches of extreme bulldust and big holes," and while I've no idea what extreme bulldust is, I'm pretty *au fait* with the concept of a big hole. The vehicle rental people were very clear on the subject. While we were doing them a favour – relocating their vehicle from one side of Australia to another – for which there would be no charge, other than fuel, there would be hell to pay if we put the van in a big hole on the Plenty Highway. Stick to tarmac was the strong advice.

Besides, there were good reasons for sticking to the tarmac, driving north and turning right, the first being the chance to stop off at the Devil's Marbles, around a four-hour drive north of Alice. These are huge, circular granite boulders – twice the size of a person, or even bigger – that are spread across a wide, shallow valley, just off the highway.

There are all sorts of boring reasons why they exist – sorry, geologists – to do with the relative durability of the land's layers of sandstone and granite, and erosion over several millennia, but such dullness was never going to get a look-in when it came to naming them. The minute you clap eyes on the boulders, you can see why nineteenth-century European explorers called them 'marbles.' Apparently rolled across the landscape, they lie jumbled together in groups, some precariously balanced, others cracked and eroded, and even split down the middle in some cases.

Like all such places in Australia, it's also a sacred Aboriginal site with important spiritual and ceremonial connections – the Waramungu people know it as Karlu Karlu, which sounds suitably mellifluous and meaningful until you discover that *karlu karlu* just means "round boulders." The Waramungu, I suspect, were just having a laugh at the Europeans when they came up with that.

We followed the trail, clambered around inappropriately and snapped a few photos, in the perfunctory way that tourists do at a site whose cultural significance they can't possibly understand, and then drove off north towards Tennant Creek.

The only proper town before the right turn to Brisbane, Tennant Creek was our first-night stop, after three hundred miles on the road. I was very excited by this, because of a story I once heard about a fellow travel writer's visit to the town during their annual festival.

It's not like he'd gone there expecting high culture. Tennant Creek, you'll understand, is an old cattle drovers' and gold-rush town, a rufty-tufty outback place of yore with an edgy reputation even now. String quartets and artisan cheese emporiums, there are not. I'd fear for a visiting hipster. About the barrel-scraping best that can be said about it is that it's the seventh-largest town in the Northern Territory – and it doesn't have to try hard for that number seven spot, seeing as the eighth-largest town only has a couple of thousand people.

Nonetheless, the official Tennant Creek website claims it's a "stopover full of surprises," though they probably don't mean the sort of surprise our writer had, when he went to the pub in the middle of the afternoon for a cool drink before doing some more travel-writing stuff. The long, stainless-steel bar was being sluiced down with water when he arrived, not for hygiene purposes – which would have been disturbing enough – but so that the annual Bar-Belly-Sliding Competition could take place. Fearsomely large Australian gentlemen in skimpy shorts – with mullets a-flowing – took it in turns to propel themselves belly-down along the bar, with the winner being the one who could slide himself right off the end without assistance.

You can see why anyone would be excited about a trip to Tennant Creek, but all I can say is that, outside belly-slide time, it does not make the heart sing. As outback towns go, it's fairly typical, with a wide, tree-lined main street of drive-up shops selling everything from slabs of meat to bush hats, and with a bit of suburban sprawl either side. A few thousand people live there, and if you had some spare time you could visit a couple of museums and the cultural centre. But we'd already driven a long way and all we really wanted was a meal and a bed for the night, which was largely the point of Tennant Creek for intrepid travellers such as ourselves.

Not too intrepid, mind. We may have been driving a campervan, but driving was all I planned to do in it. After a first day of barrelling along the hot, dusty Stuart Highway in an oven-like vehicle, there was no prospect of me wanting to sleep in it as well, never mind wash and cook. What were we, hobos?

"But what would Steve Irwin do?" she said, in a final attempt to point out the absurdity of driving a campervan for thousands of miles without ever camping in it.

"Steve would camp by a billabong and boil a billy by a coolibah tree," I said. "But Steve also knows how to wrestle crocodiles, and we don't. And what about the killer spiders that live in the toilets? Australia is famous for its toilet-dwelling killer spiders. Every campground is bound to be full of them."

"Motel then?" she said.

"Excellent idea. Let's just pretend we're driving a regular van. We don't even have to look in the back at the beds and stove, and all that stuff. We'll say we never noticed them."

Back on the road the next morning, it was a quick fifteen-mile drive north of town to the famed right turn at Threeways, where the Barkly Highway cuts eastwards towards Queensland and the driving becomes a whole lot more serious. Quite how serious, you can tell from the road sign at the junction, which only has one destination marked on it – the town of Mount Isa, four hundred miles away. That's a lot of driving through desert scrub on ruler-straight stretches of road, with nothing to stop for save the very occasional roadhouse, where you can fill up on fuel and Aussie meat pies.

The highway is also the only tarmac road which runs west to east, which makes it a major transport route for the multiple freight trailers known as road trains. Knowledge of the size and scale of British delivery vehicles – say a Tesco's supermarket truck – will be of no help to the unsuspecting driver. If you're pootling along in a campervan, marvelling at the endless monotony of the stumpy trees and red dust, then the sudden appearance of a hundred-and-fifty-foot-long road train coming up fast behind you on the narrow black-top is a rare treat for the old heart. They could prescribe it on the NHS, such is its tachycardiac effect.

"What are you doing?" she said.

"Trying not to panic and hoping it will overtake us, because otherwise we've got to drive at about a hundred miles an hour to stay in front of it, and trust that the petrol doesn't run out."

"Isn't that dangerous? If it overtakes us?"

"I'm assuming so, from the loud and repeated honking noises."

"Well, slow down and pull over then," she said.

But I wasn't about to do that because I had read the advice that said, under no circumstances should you slow down until the overtaking road train has fully moved over to the other lane. There had been liberal use of the word 'sideswiped,' which is not really a word you want to read in a set of driving safety instructions.

I'd like to say that I handled the situation with aplomb, though it's probably more accurate to imagine a scene from the new movie *Mr Bean Meets Mad Max*, with me in the Rowan Atkinson role and our friendly, honking truckie as Mel Gibson. Less *Fury Road* and more *Feck-Me Road*; you get the picture.

I couldn't tell you what happened exactly, but some minutes – or possibly hours – later, I now had a road train in front of me, rather than behind me, and a river of sweat that started on the crown of my head and gushed down my back, pooled around my thighs and poured into my shoes. We drove on, alternately squelching and not speaking about the matter, which seemed like the best thing to do under the circumstances.

Another day's outback drive put us across the border into Queensland, ever closer to Mount Isa. Any initial temptation to try and make it from Tennant Creek in a day had been tempered by the sheer slog of driving on a remote road with very little in the way of distraction.

You start off thinking how exciting it is, to be driving across a continent, but after a few hours of straight-ahead steering, dusty roadsides, red dirt and wispy bushes, you find your mind wandering, which is not at all safe because Australia is ridiculous. If you veered off the side of a country road in England, you might take out a molehill or two. The outback equivalent is the termite mound – towers of clay, soil and sand, bound together by termite saliva, that can stand over ten feet high. There might be a million termites in one of those things. Knocking over their home doesn't seem like a good idea. They'd be cross, I expect, times a million.

It's also not advisable to drive in the dusk or at night because of the other only-in-Australia hazard, namely the bush kangaroo, which has a nasty habit of bounding out of the gloom and into oncoming headlights. Again, in England, the biggest thing you're likely to hit is a pheasant which, while unfortunate for the pheasant, isn't going to lead to awkward conversations with the insurance company. Kangaroos on the other hand can grow up to six feet tall, weigh over ninety kilos and – fun kangaroo fact – can't move backwards to get out of the way. Speeding vehicle vs roo, there are no winners, and as no one wanted Skippy embedded in the front of the van, we took it easy. We only drove in daylight, spent another night en route, and rolled into Mount Isa on a baking hot afternoon, ready for a beer.

I don't know what we were expecting from a sprawling mineral-mining town and cattle-grazing centre, which is not only one of the world's biggest producers of copper, lead, silver and zinc but also known as the rodeo capital of Australia.

In the same way that it's always a bit suspicious when local tourist authorities start comparing their unheralded towns to Paris or Venice, we had to wonder at the claim that Mount Isa was a city "rich in history and culture" – bold, for a place only founded in 1923, where the big attraction is an underground mine tour. And maybe on another day – as at Tennant Creek – we'd have enjoyed it more had we hung around, explored the surroundings and soaked up the fabled sunsets. But we were tired and thirsty and, after checking in at a motel, wandered down the road to the nearest pub.

We didn't really notice its name as we pushed in through Western-style swing doors. It probably wasn't called The Muck & Drill or The Slaughtered Cow, but it certainly gave the impression of being the sort of place that would roll out a hearty welcome to a grubby miner or dusty cowhand intent on treating themselves to drinks, dinner and a punch-up. The décor and furniture, for example, was all fashioned from stainless steel. I mean *everything* – riveted floor, bar, stools, tables, chairs and wall panels. Handy for hosing down, I suppose. If there was ever a venue for bar-belly sliding, this was it.

Ordering a beer in Australia is fraught with confusion at the best of times. Depending on which part of the country you're in, ask for a simple beer and someone is likely to say something impenetrable like, "Schooner of VB, all right?" or "Stubby OK, mate?"

You've no idea what they are talking about, so you simply nod and end up with an amber fluid the temperature of liquid nitrogen, served in a vessel that could be the size of a thimble or a bucket. Here, in The Shovel & Stun Gun, there was also the considerable danger of revealing our national identities with one ill-chosen phrase. They say it's not a slur, but it's hard to hear the question, "Bloody Pom, are ya?", as anything but a robust challenge and, in a Mount Isa pub, the less fighting talk, the better, I'd say.

We needn't have worried, on account of the limited range of drinks available at The Excavator & Abbatoir. Presumably working on the assumption that, what else were we going to order, the barman had two frothy beers waiting for us by the time we got across the room. Under the gaze of several dusty, wild-eyed men in singlets we took them to one of those high, round bar tables with matching bar stools, where we discovered another endearing fact about the place. Not only was everything made from stainless steel, the tables and stools were all bolted to the floor, presumably to make a fairer contest of the fights later on in the evening. Consequently, we couldn't move the stools closer to the table and instead, sat there, marooned about a yard adrift, holding drinks that were by now freezing the very blood in our fingers.

"Don't catch anyone's eye, and don't ask me what Steve Irwin would do," I said.

"I think one of those men *is* Steve Irwin. He has the same singlet, with stains that you could only get from wrenching the back teeth from a crocodile."

"I take it we are not dining at this establishment? There are pies."

"We are not. You drink your beer *and* mine, I'd like to keep my larynx, and then we'll leave when no one's looking."

We sloped out of the pub and then, next morning, out of Mount Isa too. Ahead, another eight straight hours of outback driving as far as the cattle town of Longreach, after which if the end wasn't exactly in sight, it would at least only be about seven hundred miles away.

That seemed something to hang on to, as the tarmac stretched out ahead and the red dirt disappeared off into the horizon.

About three hours out of Mount Isa we stopped at the tiny town of McKinlay, where the roadside pub is an obligatory port of call, being the place that featured in the first *Crocodile Dundee* movie. It was only named the Walkabout Creek after the film had come out – it was The Federal before that – and had since been gussied up for the tourists, but it certainly looked the part, with its shady veranda and wooden, film-set interior. That said, it's hard to escape the feeling that we only think that's what outback pubs should be like because of *Crocodile Dundee*. The one in Mount Isa was probably closer to the mark than we knew.

With Longreach eventually behind us, it was a straight shot to Rockhampton and the Queensland coast, but that still meant over four hundred miles of dusty driving. The route passed through more small, isolated, rural townships, forgettable places whose names were more evocative than the towns themselves – Barcaldine, Jericho, Alpha, Emerald.

Finally, at Rockhampton, another right turn and we were en route for Brisbane, with a few beach stops on the way to shake the dust and aches from our bodies. We had to admit, as we dipped our feet in the water somewhere on the Sunshine Coast, that this was nice. Blue skies, palm trees, warm ocean; not desert scrub, red rocks and termite mounds.

Even so, there was much to miss from our outback

drive, from the mesmerising, traffic-free panoramas to the star-filled skies. At the time, it had seemed hard-going and never-ending, but despite the monotony of the roads, it had never been boring. How else would we have had the chance to visit the seventh-largest town in the Northern Territory or the scariest pub in Queensland? On what other trip could I have played chicken with a two-hundred-tonne articulated truck?

Best of all, there was still Steve Irwin to come, or at least his Australia Zoo at Beerwah, about an hour north of Brisbane. If you've been intrigued so far by mentions of the great man, I hope it's not a terrible spoiler to reveal that Steve sadly died back in 2006, about five years after our visit. He also died in the most Steve-Irwin way possible, which was by being stung by a stingray while snorkelling on the Great Barrier Reef. That's like David Attenborough being eaten by a silverback gorilla – you know it's tragic but also you can't say you're entirely surprised, given that Steve's working day usually consisted of him prising open the jaws of a fifteen-foot croc and saying "Crikey!"

We didn't expect to see Steve that day at the zoo, because he was often away filming, but it was enough to be on the hallowed ground. And as the zoo is still in the hands of the family, with Steve and his image looming large everywhere you go, even today it's a thrill to visit if you like to see young, bouncy, tanned Australians handling dangerous wildlife.

We parked up the van one final time – still defiantly un-camped in – and headed straight for the zoo's showpiece 'Crocoseum,' where they put on a daily show featuring the saltwater crocodile, the largest, fiercest reptile on the planet. They grow to over twenty feet long, can hide underwater holding their breath for up to seven hours, and leap out to tackle prey as big as a kangaroo or buffalo.

Like the termites, the toilet-spiders and the three-foot lizards, the lurking croc is just a ridiculous thing to have to worry about while going around Australia minding your own business. But after surviving more than two thousand miles on the road, we thought we could handle it. And if not, there was someone trained by Steve Irwin on hand to do the wrestling for us – we could always chip in with the Crikeys if necessary.

WASTING TIME AND MONEY IN YORKSHIRE

"Notice anything odd about the toast?" said Ian, who is a barrister and therefore professionally trained in spotting funny business.

"Heart-shaped?" I said.

"Indeed. What would Captain Cook have made of this?"

"It's hard to say. I doubt he would have approved. Ship's cook would surely have been risking a flogging, serving up anything except hard tack."

We were on day one of our winter walk on the trail of England's most famous navigator/New World discoverer/violent colonial oppressor, take your pick, and breakfast was being served. The idea was to hike twenty miles along the North Sea coast, from Saltburn-by-the-Sea to Whitby, partly to seek out historic traces of the Captain and partly, well mostly, to drink beer in seaside pubs and talk over old times.

It turned out, early on, that scant traces were all that

were left when it came to following the Captain Cook trail. The previous day, we had poked around the nearby village of Great Ayton, where the young James moved with his family when he was eight years old. It's a handsome place, with a village green and a rushing river, and they are pretty keen on the Cook connection, which explains the presence of a statue of the great man, or rather the teenager that he was when he lived in Great Ayton. If you've only ever seen the renowned images of Cook posed in a naval uniform, surrounded by maps, then I can heartily recommend this portrayal – a ripped, bare-chested teenager with flowing, wind-blown locks. The sculptor had clearly been watching *The Beach* during chisel breaks.

James went to the village school and the schoolroom was still there, now a museum, but it was a modern reconstruction. There was no trace, either, of the long-lost family home up on the moors at Aireyholme Farm, where Cook's father had been the farm manager. There is a building called Cook's Cottage that was verifiably owned by his parents, but James himself never lived in it – and you can't see it in any case, at least not in Great Ayton, because it was transported brick by brick in the 1930s to Melbourne, Australia, of all places. And there's a towering obelisk on a nearby hill, called Captain Cook's Monument, raised fifty years after his death and featuring a very unhelpful plaque that talks about spreading civilisation to 'pagan and savage tribes,' which doesn't exactly read well these days.

All in all, it had been a day of wet, moorland

tramping and slim pickings, but a comfortable night in a country-house hotel had gone some way to making amends. A quiet night, a roaring fire in the lounge, a stiff brandy before bed, and an early night. Next up was the eight or nine miles along the cliffs to the fishing village of Staithes, where according to the guidebook, James moved when he was sixteen to work in a grocer's shop.

The toast was a puzzle, though. Who cuts breakfast toast into heart shapes?

"Enjoyed your stay, gentlemen?" said the receptionist. "Here, let me fetch your bill," at which point things became much clearer.

It was very reasonable; indeed, a bargain, which is why we'd booked it in the first place. Dinner, bed and breakfast for two people at a hugely discounted winter rate – or, as the bill had it, '1 x Romantic Treat for a Valentine's Couple.'

"Ah," said Ian. "The roses at dinner."

"And the red cushions embroidered with the word 'Love' on the pushed-together twin beds."

"You'd think we'd have noticed, what with you being a top travel writer with a keen eye for detail."

"And with you being a top barrister with a forensic nose for funny business."

"Well, everyone's been very welcoming. I'd come here again for a romantic treat, any day."

We hoisted backpacks and hiked out to the seafront at Saltburn and then up onto the cliffs. It was a grim, grey day, with low clouds hanging over a grim, grey North Sea – not exactly Valentine's weather, but entirely to be expected in a North Yorkshire winter. There's a fair amount of guff written – some of it, probably by me – about the fact that the young James Cook must have wandered the moors, looking out over the distant waves and dreaming of a future life at sea.

Well, I can tell you, there's absolutely nothing in a February North Sea view that's remotely encouraging of a career change. One look at the icy, muddy depths and the indistinct horizon and you'd be pulling your smock tight and thinking that being a farmhand wasn't so bad. You'd be weighing up freezing cold water and heavy, wet clothes on one hand, and a straw-filled barn with piles of steaming cow dung on the other, and coming down on the side of the poop every time.

"It's probably why he wanted to work in a shop," said Ian, as we walked headlong into a cutting wind. "I don't think he wanted to go to sea at all. Why would you? It's wet and cold. Whereas in a grocer's shop there will be a fire and biscuits."

The shop under discussion was in Staithes, which meant following the coastal path through driving rain up and over Boulby Cliff, trumpeted as the highest cliff on the eastern coast of England – which, once you dig down into the particulars (just England, just the east coast), isn't as impressive as it sounds. Still, in a slippery, muddy winter, with sea fog swirling around, it's six hundred and sixty-six feet you'd rather be on top of than falling off, so we picked our way with care.

There's actually more impressive stuff going on under the cliff, as below our feet was Boulby Mine, where they've been digging out potash and polyhalite (used as fertilisers) since the 1960s. That's not the interesting bit – sorry again, geologists – rather the mine itself, where there are now over six hundred miles of tunnels, caverns and roads beneath the surface, buried so deep that it's an ideal place for an underground laboratory.

Here, in something I'm imagining – with no evidence – that looks like a mad doctor's secret science bunker, they are searching for Dark Matter, the hypothetical missing matter that's reckoned to make up eighty-five percent of the universe. Protected by three and a half thousand feet of rock above them, the white-coated, bespectacled, boggle-eyed, fly-away haired boffins – again, no evidence – can screen out the natural cosmic rays and look for the dark stuff until the cows come home. They probably have little robot assistants and everything. When the full story of the universe is told, Staithes will have played its part. It makes you think, or it would if you weren't busy concentrating on not walking off the edge of a cliff or falling down a mine.

Fair play to Staithes when we finally got there. It's a hugely atmospheric village with a cobbled main street lined with Georgian buildings and a sheltered harbour overlooked by higgledy-piggledy houses and a seafront pub. It would have been lovely under a shaft or two of sunlight, but even in the wintry gloom it was easy to see that this was a place of charm and character.

There were stepped alleys lined with white-painted buildings, and terraces higher up from where there were sneaky peeks to the sea and the sky. Nonetheless, living there, you suspect, is a challenge, given that when we finally tracked down the building claiming to be Cook's shop, near the harbour, it became clear that, yet again, there was only a tenuous connection.

"Because," said Ian, "it says here that the original shop was washed into the sea."

We looked at the shop and then out across the harbour walls, about two hundred yards away.

"That's quite a way to be washed."

"The pub's been damaged by waves three times, too. This seems a rather dangerous place to start a business."

"I'm amending your theory," I said. "I think Cook did want to work in a shop, and then he came here and discovered that he might as well go to sea, what with the constant washing away. At least a ship is supposed to be on the water. You'd be prepared for the waves. Unlike behind a counter in a shop. There, waves would be a surprise."

"Pub?"

"All right, but let's sit near the door. In case, you know, waves."

"So far," said Ian later, nursing a pint, "there has been a disappointing amount of actual Cook-related sights. I blame the guidebook writers for overstating the evidence."

"I'm a guidebook writer."

"Then I blame you. Nothing, so far, has been worth seeing. Staithes is very nice, but I don't think we'd have come if some guidebook writer hadn't banged on about the Captain Cook connections. Great Ayton, also very nice, but tramping around on the moors looking for non-existent cottages and racist obelisks was a waste of time."

"You seem very concerned about it all? Have you not accepted and transcended?"

"I'm living in the moment," said Ian. "I'm sitting in a pub that may be washed away at any minute. I'm also allowed to express an opinion."

"We have to write about the history," I said. "It's part of the attraction of a place. Not everywhere can have the Parthenon or the pyramids. Even traces and echoes can be interesting. I thought you'd enjoy the historical associations."

"Staithes has a building that is on the site of another building that was washed away, that James Cook once spent ten minutes in, hiding from the waves and eating biscuits. That's not proper history."

"Then what do you suggest?"

"Funny you should ask," said Ian. "I have an idea for a new kind of guidebook."

He outlined the concept and we developed it further on the next day's walk, as we tramped over the cliffs to the sheltered village and long, sandy beach at Runswick Bay. It went like this.

Instead of waxing lyrically about museums, sights and attractions of dubious interest, our new guidebook would apply a rating system based on whether – in our professional opinion – something was a Waste of Time (WT) or a Waste of Money (WM). In some cases – a terrible attraction that you also had to pay to get into, or which cost a lot to reach – something might be a Waste of Time *and* Money (WTM). In order to provide some comparative context, there would also be a sliding scale of wastefulness, so that sights and attractions might be rated an Utter Waste of Time (UWT) or Money (UWM) or even, in some circumstances, a Complete and Utter Waste of Time (CUWT) or Money (CUWM).

Only the most egregious examples would earn the highest accolade we could bestow – an attraction so devoid of interest, and so expensive to visit, that it would be flagged as a CUWTM.

"How about establishing some benchmarks? What about Stonehenge?"

"A load of big stones that you can't get particularly close to," said Ian. "But you can see them from the road for free as you drive past. So, only an Utter Waste of Time."

"Loch Ness?"

"Big lake, nothing in it, expensive cruise to confirm that there's nothing in it. Utter Waste of Time and Money."

"Eiffel Tower?"

"Ah well, depends. If all you do is go and look at it, then borderline WT. It is quite big and impressive after all. But if you stand in a queue for ages, pay a fortune to go up it and then realise that the only decent view in Paris is *of* the Eiffel Tower, which you now can't see because you're up it, then CUWTM."

"All right then. Cook's shop in Staithes?"

"WT only, surely? Not a penny spent, and we were walking this way anyway."

We arrived in Runswick Bay as the rain lashed across the beach, which was being thrashed by grey waves that pummelled the clay cliffs behind. This, too, seemed the sort of place that would benefit from some blue skies and fluffy clouds. A tight-knit huddle of red-roofed houses curled up behind the harbour, and from a terrace outside the only pub, high on the hill, there would have been a fine view on a sunny day. The beach is wide and sandy, too, which is a rarity on this coast, and in the cliffs behind have been excavated some extraordinary Jurassic-age marine fossils. They seemed like good reasons to come back another time when it wasn't raining. Indeed, it was hard to believe on a winter's day, but two hundred million years ago this whole area lay under a warm, shallow ocean and later became a temperate coastal area of scrub and forest. Geologically, historically and technically, you could prob-ably describe Runswick Bay as 'tropical' and not be sued.

We climbed back onto the cliffs and followed the trail around the bay and past Kettleness, where – no surprise by this time – there had been more washing away. In fact, the whole of the original village had simply fallen into the sea one night in 1829, which would have perplexed the postman the next morning.

By the time we reached Sandsend, a couple of miles further on, the weather had begun to lift. It had stopped raining and there was a hint of lighter grey in the sky, which is considered positively equatorial in the North Yorkshire winter. Turning inland slightly to cross the river and then rounding the corner, suddenly the beach stretched out ahead, with Whitby visible in the distance, three miles away.

"James Cook came here in 1746, to be apprenticed to Quaker ship-owners. Whitby has many reminders of Cook's early maritime life."

"Says the guidebook?" said Ian.

"Says history."

"Yes, well, that may be. I'm reserving judgement."

"You're reserving judgement on history?"

"I am. I shall be judging history on the basis of the new guidebook rating method. Lead on."

We dumped our packs in our hotel for the night, an eighteenth-century coaching inn on the cobbled main street of the old town, and went looking for James Cook, which is easier in Whitby than anywhere else in England. He was only a young man when he lived here too – just for a few years, while he learned his trade – but the town doesn't let that bother it in the slightest. You get the feeling it would happily rename itself Cooktown, if only a pesky town in northern Queensland, Australia, hadn't got there first. As it is, there's a striking monument high on the West Cliff and a full-scale replica of his most famous ship, the *Endeavour*, moored at the harbour. And best of all, there's the original ship-owner's building where he first lodged as an apprentice, now the Captain Cook Memorial Museum.

"The actual building?"

"So it seems."

"Not a replacement for one that was washed away?"

"Indeed, no. It is the only surviving building that can definitely be connected to Cook."

"Says the guidebook?"

"Says everyone. It is a fact of history."

We spent time and money exploring the museum, which turned out to be not a waste of either. In fact, it was delightful. Preserved as a typical, well-to-do house of the period, there was plenty of authenticity, from the original floorboards, doors and hand-carved staircase to the roof beams fashioned from old ships' timbers. There are maps, charts and model ships, and letters, artefacts and original documents, such as the note of condolence written by King George III when Cook's wife, Margaret, died. Meanwhile, up in the attic is where young James did actually sleep, squashed in together with the other apprentices, learning the ropes in mathematics, navigation and astronomy while he helped sail coal-ships up and down the English coast.

We left Whitby the next day, and left Cook to his youthful endeavours. The whole of his fame or notoriety, take your pick, was still to come, while he walked the streets and sailed the harbour of a town that he'd largely recognise, even today. The cobbled alleys, the steep steps up to the ruined clifftop abbey, the swirling waters beyond the pincered twin piers – there are few more atmospheric coastal towns in England than Whitby and Cook is just the icing on the cake.

There was a last breakfast to negotiate, which was in apparent danger of receiving a WM rating.

"Pray, why? Seems very nice."

"Notice anything odd about the toast?" said Ian.

"Not heart-shaped, you mean?"

"Precisely. I am not feeling the Romantic Retreat vibe."

"If I have to judge the shape of the toast in every hotel I stay in, from now on, I'll never finish writing another guidebook."

"A loss to the world, I'm sure. It is" – said Ian, who is a barrister, and therefore brimming with such phrases – "entirely a matter for you."

PERMISSION TO LAND IN LUXOR

CALL ME OLD-FASHIONED, but you'd better have a good reason for planning on waking me up at four in the morning.

"The winds are calmest at dawn," said the travel agent, tapping his nose, in the manner of a spy announcing his arrival at a secret location.

"And the balloon is less likely to have an accident then," he added, which was not the clinching detail he thought it was.

But I did want to see the temples of Karnak and Luxor from the air, more than I feared being smeared across the ground in the Valley of the Kings, so I signed the various waivers and set my alarm clock. Four o'clock it was.

Hot-air ballooning in Luxor is a big attraction, but it doesn't have the greatest safety record. Balloons in Egypt have crashed, caught fire, hit cables and flown into things at reasonably regular intervals over the years, but then again, what does anyone expect? They are massive nylon globes with a wicker basket underneath, powered by combustible gas cylinders that emit a roaring flame. They don't have brakes or a steering wheel and rely on wind currents for manoeuvring. I'm no scientist, but they don't seem like a good bet for a trouble-free ride. It's amazing any of them go up and come down again without incident. I should think you only need a one and a zero for the "Days without an accident" counter in your average hot-air-balloon office.

As it is, I don't like flying at the best of times, which is not helpful for a travel writer. I used to be all right until the time they thought they had found a bomb on board a flight I was on, and we had to make an emergency landing in Iran. After that, funnily enough, I became less keen on the whole flying business. I usually apply copious amounts of alcohol, and work on the basis that any aircraft I'm on is bound to crash, so that I'm pleasantly surprised if terribly hungover when it doesn't.

I take the train where I can. But if the promise outweighs the fear, I'll go for it. To visit Australia again, I know I'll have to fly – they just better keep that drinks trolley fully stocked. If, to see the Niagara Falls up close, I must get on a flimsy looking helicopter, so be it. Not that I saw the Niagara Falls up close, you understand, because as soon as the pilot put the helicopter into a deep dive "for a better look," I shrank into my seat, whimpered uncontrollably, and didn't open my eyes again until we landed twenty minutes later. Big waterfall, apparently, meant to be quite impressive.

I figured a balloon ride over Luxor, while inherently dangerous, would be – counter-intuitively – safer. No rotors, no moving parts, for a start. I have never been fully convinced that an aeroplane's wings aren't just screwed on to the fuselage with a three-quarter-inch metal thread, so the thick, knotted ropes attaching the balloon basket already seemed far more secure. And how high could a balloon possibly go? You could probably jump out and land in the Nile if you had to. I was entirely happy with this delusional risk assessment because I really, really wanted to see the Luxor temples from the air.

I'd already seen them from the ground, along with everyone else, and because it was summer it had been the usual exhausting experience for anyone visiting the famed ancient capital of Upper Egypt. Once known as Thebes, the pharaohs' capital, the 'City of a Hundred Gates', Luxor sits on the banks of the River Nile and is nothing so much as an open-air museum of extraordinary richness. Century upon century, layer upon layer. For sheer archaeological spectacle, there's no place like it anywhere else on the planet. But touring the sights can be brutal.

In daytime temperatures approaching forty degrees Celsius, we had trailed around the Great Temple at Karnak and then skulked in the cool, labyrinthine tombs which puncture the barren hills of the Valley of the Kings. We'd crocodiled through countless chambers of vivid hieroglyphics, walked between towering stone columns, and listened to an endless litany of kings and dynasties that made less sense the longer the day went on. The scale and scope – thousands of years old, hundreds of feet high, built by countless, unnamed workers – was almost beyond comprehension. In addition, guides, touts, stallholders and itinerant sellers had all had a piece of us. Souvenirs had been thrust, threatened, waved, offered, proffered, brandished and even bought. We'd 'done' Luxor and Luxor had done us.

What I really needed was sleep, not a crack-of-dawn alarm call. But what I also wanted was a second go at Luxor, from the air, without the heat and hassle. So four o'clock it was, which – to be strictly accurate – is not the crack of dawn at all. Dawn implies the imminent promise of some sun. Let's call it what it is and have done with it. If you want to go ballooning in Egypt, you need to get up in the middle of the night.

By four-thirty we were down by the Nile, where it was at least blessedly cool – the first time in days that I had been able to breathe properly outdoors. We were given a cup of tea and a croissant – they said breakfast, I thought midnight snack – and away we went. Crossing to the West Bank in an open launch, the shadows began to lift from Luxor's buildings, and I could just about make out the reed-strewn banks on the other side. It was quiet apart from the chug of the engine and the occasional call of a bird that had got up too early.

At the launch site, we were introduced to our pilot, who had the unlikely Arabic name of Kevin and turned out to be Scottish. I liked Kevin immediately, mostly because he wore a crisp, white shirt with gold epaulettes and a peaked cap – clearly a man who knew a thing or two about reassuring jittery, sleep-deprived customers that they were in safe hands, despite the fact they were about to be herded into a crate hanging off a giant, flammable plastic bag.

Kevin came with a ground crew, who jumped out of a pick-up truck and started laying out the balloon and connecting the basket and fuel cylinders. To say they were a cheery bunch would be an understatement. It was like being in a scene from *Madagascar*: as the sun finally began to rise, they all began to sing loudly, banging out a rhythm on the sides of the truck. Kevin, meanwhile, stood some distance away, checking the winds, which seemed to the layman to consist of looking at his watch and sticking a finger in the air. But the man had epaulettes and a pilot's cap, so we left him to it while the crew liked to move it, move it.

By about six a.m. the balloon was ready, swaying above the ground, with the basket tethered to the truck to stop it lifting off prematurely. Unless the truck was coming too, always a possibility.

The balloon basket had high sides and four or five compartments inside. Kevin did a bit of professional sizing-up and distributed us around the basket, either according to weight or dependent on who he thought was most likely to panic – get the whimperers in the middle, that would be my guess.

It was all done very calmly and unobtrusively, which I can tell you from experience is a far better method than that used when I went on a sightseeing light-aircraft flight over Canyonlands in Utah. To be fair to that pilot, he'd already bristled when we asked him where his dad was when he walked up to the plane. Pro pilot tip, if you look *that* young, you should probably go for a false moustache or something. Then he reached into his bag, pulled out a set of bathroom scales and weighed every passenger before seating us in strict order. Knowing that the aircraft tolerances are *that* wafer-thin does not fill you full of confidence, especially when you're in the hands of a pilot who might want his mummy at any minute.

Kevin, though, was a man in command. He took up a position in the middle, had a quick look around, reached into his pocket for a two-way radio and requested clearance from Luxor airport.

Nice one, Kev, we thought. Good joke: pilot's uniform *and* a radio.

But after a short silence came a squawk and the rasping voice of an Egyptian air-traffic controller giving us permission to ascend to eight hundred feet, so that showed us.

Up we went. Not in a roaring rush of wind, as you might expect, but slowly, in gently bobbing rises, until the singing, waving ground crew was out of earshot. You barely felt the balloon lift. One minute, ground; next minute, sky; and no real way to determine how high we were, with just a featureless plain below. With short blasts from the gas cylinders, Kevin positioned us in an airstream and then switched off.

Eight hundred feet up, hands gripping the waist-high

basket sides, everyone peered down onto a timeless Egyptian landscape. It was utterly silent in the dawn light. Below, was the Valley of the Kings, now ochre-red as the morning sun rose; then the rock-cut mortuary temple of Hatshepsut; and the sandstone figures of the Colossi of Memnon, all laid out like markers on a desert map. Overwhelming from the ground, from up high they were suddenly human in scale – Shelley's mighty works in 'Ozymandias', reduced by Kevin and his balloon to a scene "where the lone and level sands stretch far away."

The line between parched desert and cultivated land was abrupt – on one side grey and red, the other green. We drifted towards the Nile across chequered, irrigated fields, watching birds wheeling hundreds of feet below us. Occasionally, the balloon would rise or fall as Kevin looked for a new air current to change the direction of flight, and he followed the river to put us directly above the Karnak and Luxor temple complexes, two hours before the day's tourists arrived to trudge around. The searing sun of yesterday, the heavy-footed walk, the tired minds overloaded with facts – all forgotten as we floated serenely by.

On the outskirts of town, we dropped down far enough to make out individual flat-roofed houses, whose enclosed yards contained chicken runs and chained dogs that were asleep in the dirt. Just below us, almost close enough to touch, a household woke up. From a line of beds on the roof there were stirrings under white cotton sheets and then an entire family in night-shirts was waving as we drifted over their house. Did they do this every day? Were they on the balloon company's payroll? Anything is possible I suppose, but I like to think that there's a middle-aged man in Luxor who still remembers the time his dad woke him up when a hot-air balloon flew over their house.

The flight finally ended in the fields beyond, but not before an exciting segment where the ground crew suddenly reappeared in the pick-up and chased us as we descended. They were still singing, but we'd now gone from *Madagascar* to the Keystone Cops, as they careered through sugar cane fields, trying to anticipate the landing zone. At some point, we picked up a gaggle of shrieking children too, which added to the hilarity as the balloon skimmed along horizontally, ten feet above the ground. I must have missed the bit where Kevin requested permission to land from the control tower, though to be fair to the Luxor airport authorities they were probably more concerned with keeping an eye on their runways rather than random farmers' fields.

Everyone hauled on the guy ropes at the given signal, the basket bounded a couple of times in the crops, and at last we were all bundled out on to firm ground. Turns out there are brakes, after all, though you're a bit more personally involved in landing the craft than is strictly encouraging for a nervous flyer. Can't quite imagine the Qantas pilot letting everyone from rows one through twelve have a go with the joystick, but Kevin was nothing if not inclusive and I am now officially allowed to say that I have landed a hot-air balloon. There were handshakes all round as we got in the vehicle to take us back to town. I'm not sure, but Kevin may even have saluted.

After all that excitement, it was only seven a.m. Still not getting-up time, but nonetheless, Luxor redeemed itself from on high – a good enough reason after all to set the alarm for the middle of the night.

CAPITAL PUNISHMENT IN MONTENEGRO

ALL ROADS LEAD TO ROME, it is said. Which is quite all right, because Rome has an eternal beauty and is the sort of place you fall in love with at first sight. You wouldn't mind the roads leading you to Rome; no complaints there on the road-leading front.

However, the jury's out on the Balkan nation of Montenegro and its capital city, Podgorica. It's only Rome-like in that it's very difficult to avoid, travelling from east to west or north to south, as the highways and buses invariably contrive to deposit you there whether you want to go or not. And – as you gaze around the bus station, idly wondering how it is that you have ended up in a city you can't quite pronounce (try Pod-gor-eetsa) – I might as well be clear about your prospects.

You are not going to fall in love. Not with the city, at any rate. A flirtation or a drunken one-night stand, very possibly, since there are some great bars and restaurants, but as a capital city Podgorica is a loveless mystery wrapped in a romantic disappointment. A feature in the *Guardian* questioned whether it was "the most boring city in Europe?" and the question mark was probably a sub-editor's attempt to be kind.

"How come it's like it is?" is a better question.

Settled for at least two thousand years as a city, it's not like Podgorica doesn't have history on its side. The mighty imperial forces of Rome, Turkey and Austria-Hungary all did the usual trick of marching in, knocking down and building up, but whatever was architecturally distinctive about Podgorica disappeared in the cata-clysmic bombing of World War II as the Allies drove Germany and Italy from the Balkans.

The city was collateral damage as Europe was re-ordered after the war. As part of the new Yugoslavia, Podgorica was declared capital of the Republic of Montenegro in 1948 – replacing the old royal capital of Cetinje – and then renamed Titograd, after the Yugoslav president, Josip Broz Tito. It was rebuilt pretty much from the ground up in the 1950s and 1960s in a typical flourish of regimented Eastern Bloc design. It finally became capital of a newly independent Montenegro in 2006, and thus claims the distinction of being one of the world's most recently declared capital cities.

All that history doesn't make modern-day Podgorica boring, but – risen from the ashes of war – it does make it hard to like.

The small city centre – population still only around a couple of hundred thousand – is one of mundane, high-rise apartment blocks, gridded streets and concrete squares, built with little aesthetic appreciation. There aren't any extensive, old neighbourhoods to explore, the surviving historic sites are few and far between, and it's baking hot in summer – high thirties Celsius – which soon puts paid to lazy wanders and curious strolls.

Naturally, being – erm – an experienced travel writer, I didn't know any of this before visiting and had booked in to stay for four nights. Believe me, that is three nights longer than is strictly required to see Podgorica, but it does mean I now speak with some authority when it comes to pint-sized, post-Socialist capital cities.

I set off on the first morning to see the sights, and it's entirely possible that my judgement of the city was impaired from the outset, on account of me being half-drunk. Not from the night before, how very dare you, nothing so seedy. Instead, I had an early encounter with what the Montenegrins think of as hospitality in the shape of a couple of large shots of *rakija*, a distilled, fruit-based firewater that is pressed upon guests at every opportunity. It's impossible to avoid – all I'd done was pass the apartment host in the corridor and next thing I knew I was sitting on his balcony at nine a.m., sampling something fearsome and homemade that he referred to as "the devil's brew."

It had less a taste to it and more a physical force; a couple of drops in a fusion reactor and you could prob-ably power the city. My host poured me two chunky shots, one after the other, when I made the schoolboy error of downing the first one quickly to get it over with.

"You come here every morning," he said. "We drink,

it's traditional," which sounded like the sort of throw-away thing you might say to a tourist, except that he took his duties very seriously. If he heard the slightest footstep in the corridor, he'd be out brandishing the bottle, day or night. He was like Burt Kwouk in the *Pink Panther* films, springing out from doorways and lurking in the shadows; I virtually had to commando-roll out of the building each morning to avoid a rocket-fuelled start to the day.

Consequently, I may not have been fully on top of the initial sightseeing. This is what I can remember. There is a teeny-tiny old Ottoman quarter signalled by a rather handsome clock tower in a spacious square, a couple of mosques with slender minarets, and the very scant remnants of a riverside Turkish fortress. You could swim from a little river beach here, underneath one of the main city bridges, and when I say "you could," I mean "people do but it looks a bit grim and I wouldn't."

There is a more contemporary Millennium Bridge further along the river, built in – go figure – 2005, which lights up a bit at night. There's a boxy National Theatre and a modern, show-off Orthodox cathedral. Centre of the city, meanwhile, is Republic Square, which sounds very grand but is a charmless concrete expanse at the heart of a grid of wide shopping streets. Look it up on Tripadvisor, if you think I'm being harsh – my favourite comment, "I do not consider this a real attraction," posi-tively drips with disappointment.

It's not fair, of course, given the history and backstory, and normally I would dig a bit deeper. I'm fully prepared to believe that there's more to Podgorica than this – the map showed parks and museums for a start – but it was a skin-blistering thirty-nine degrees in August, so I wasn't inclined to tramp around in search of further diversion.

Instead, I jumped in a taxi on one of the main avenues, which resulted in the hilarity of being told by a psychic driver that it was "five euros" before I'd even given my destination. Over several days, this was the usual price wherever I wanted to go, however long or short the journey. Even so, it seemed like a bargain until the last day, when I got a taxi from the local rank outside the apartment to the train station. This was a rib-tickling "one euro," so if you're planning on seeing the sights in Podgorica by taxi, I'd start to haggle on day one.

The cab delivered me to a restaurant by the clocktower called Pod Volat, recommended by my apartment host, which was a slight worry, given his entire diet appeared to consist of fruit-based liquor.

Well, good on him, I'd go back to Podgorica any day just to eat there again, as it was an absolutely brilliant grill-house restaurant with a tree-shaded terrace that kept off the worst of the sun. There wasn't much, if any, English spoken, but there was an English-language menu, so I managed to pick out *cevapi* (mini kebabs), homemade flatbreads, red-pepper dip, and the best chips I've ever had. Hand-cut, golden, beautifully fried and piled on a platter big enough to feed four Englishmen or, apparently, one Montenegrin. The meal came with a complimentary bowl of shredded white cabbage, which everyone else dressed with salt and vinegar, and I fed to the feral cats, because please, raw cabbage when there are chips to finish?

The food was ridiculously inexpensive and very good, but the waiters were – what's the polite word? – brisk. Stuffs and fecks were not given; eyes were not caught; hand gestures were ignored. Every five minutes, one of them would come and light up a cigarette and puff away right behind me, while waiting for the kitchen to catch up with orders. Eventually, once I'd been served, the waiters abandoned me altogether, in favour of fawning over a nearby table that seemed to be occupied by local, or possibly national, celebrities of some kind. There was expressive baritone singing by a large, open-shirted, moustachioed chap – fuelled by my old friend, *rakija* – accompanied by sombre nodding along by his blinged-up associates. Then came huge amounts of applause from the entire restaurant, except me, followed by more rounds of *rakija* brought by excited waiters. This was probably the Montenegrin Tom Jones, popping in for a quiet lunch, and the Pod Volat restaurant didn't know what to do with itself.

Very well fed, much cooler by now, and no longer woozy from my breakfast *aperitif*, I began to consider the possibility that Podgorica wasn't too bad after all. (The city tourist board could do worse than use this as a strapline, by the way – 'Podgorica: Not Too Bad.' Or, come to think of it, 'Podgorica: You Could Do Worse.' It's a matter for them. I'm just a writer, what do I know about marketing?).

For a start, unlike most capital cities, it's not only

cheap but is oddly cheaper than almost anywhere else in the country, especially places such as Kotor on the coast. It might be the political, banking and administrative centre of Montenegro, but Podgorica is a bargain. Imagine it was cheaper to go on holiday to London than, say, the seaside resort of Scarborough – which, for the benefit of non-British readers, would seem very odd indeed. In actual fact, you could buy the whole town of of Scarborough for the price of a glass of wine in a fancy London bar; you'd probably even get change.

Secondly, it's convenient for lots of other places that you might want to visit, because Montenegro is only a small country. Using Podgorica as a base, you could do easy day trips by bus and train to majestic Ostrog monastery, reed-filled Lake Skadar or the haunting ruins of Stari Bar.

Or, if you'd like to see what a proper Montenegrin capital city is like, you could take the bus the hour or so over the mountains from the city to the old royal seat of Cetinje. This is everything that Podgorica isn't – a somnolent place of leafy boulevards, shady pavement cafés, green parks, handsome buildings and faded, old embassies. It's the historic, old-town atmosphere that you've been looking for, with a palpable sense of elegance and tradition. It's almost like a stage set, grand but compact, and is easy to stroll around however much *rakija* has been pressed upon you. But as all roads don't lead to Cetinje, but Podgorica, you will at least have to start in the actual modern-day capital, whatever your feelings on the subject.

In the end, Podgorica revealed itself slowly to me, mostly in the cool vaults of restaurants and shady garden-bars that served improbably large and very meaty dishes, presumably designed to soak up the booze that you've been taking on board since waking up.

The Lanterna, for example – an amiable stone-walled tavern – had a bunch of Desperate-Dan-sized grilled and deep-fried specialities, prince of which was a *Njeguski* steak – kind of like a rolled *schnitzel* stuffed with smoked ham and cheese. You don't just get one of these in a serving – oh no, the plate came with three of the monsters and after almost-but-not-quite-two I had to stop eating or I would have burst like Monty Python's Mr Creosote. I don't know how anyone has the energy to do any work in Montenegro – apart from the waiters, who all keep in trim by ferrying vast platters of meat around and smoking furiously over the guests.

After dark, when the temperature dropped, the streets around Republic Square – which I had previously dismissed as dull and boring – came into their own. Bars and restaurants took over the pavements, and people wandered in groups down the middle of the streets as traffic was halted for the night. Impromptu markets appeared, as students spread books for sale out on blankets, and bands plugged in amps on pop-up stages. Sitting outside the chic Hotel Hemera on its fan-cooled terrace, with an ice-cold Negroni, life seemed – what's the local advertising slogan? Not Too Bad.

Every night, there was a genial vibe – very local, very laidback – that provided an appealing coda to a hot-and-bothered day otherwise spent trying to fathom the hidden appeal of Podgorica.

So, there you have it. I wouldn't necessarily go there on holiday, but equally, I wouldn't avoid a night or two in Podgorica again, or even longer if I had some good day trips planned. If I'm honest, I'd go back just to have the chips in the Pod Volat.

It's a capital city quite unlike any other in Europe, that's for sure, with a look that's not entirely its fault, but comfortable in its ordinariness and happy to be left to its own devices on the Balkan fringes.

SERVING UP GROUNDNUT SOUP IN GHANA

THERE's a photograph at Mum's house of me as a baby in the arms of a handsome young man who is definitely not Dad.

It's probably been there, in the same place on a side table, for fifty years, surrounded by other photos of my sister and I at various ages. I never much noticed it or, more likely, cared about it. Who looks closely at the stuff in their parents' house? No one, that's who, not unless you want to be on the wrong end of a monologue about a great-aunt you've never heard of. In my experience, showing interest in family photos is the Russian roulette of the anecdote world – could be a straightforward answer of "That's your Uncle Arthur," could be an hour-long presentation with accompanying slides about the distaff side of the family with particular emphasis on the lack of higher educational opportunities for women in 1950s Derby.

But at some point my interest must have been piqued

– wet Sunday afternoon, nothing on TV – and I made further enquiries about why a strange man was holding me so familiarly.

"Oh yes, in the back garden," said Mum, as if that explained everything.

"Concentrate, Mother. That's not our back garden and that's not Dad. Though it is me, being cuddled by a strange man. Explain yourself."

"It's the back garden in Ghana," said Mum, which in fairness did start to explain something, because Ghana is where I was born.

"And that's Nestor," she said, again feeling that somehow covered all the bases as far as an explanation went. It's the same shorthand tactic she uses when you ask her where she's been and she says, "Oh you know, out – and all that jazz." Which would be helpful if she'd been to a jazz club, but you know it'll probably just have been the pharmacy.

Pressed further on this occasion, Mum added the bombshell clarification:

"Nestor. Our servant."

"Do tell. Are we royalty? Ooh, am I actually a prince?"

"No, he came with the house," she said, and that turned out be quite a story – at least as interesting as a re-run of *The Great Escape*, which was the alternate entertainment on offer that day.

My parents went to West Africa in 1960, when Dad got a job teaching at a secondary school in Takoradi on the Ghanaian coast. They were provided with a comfortable bungalow, full of solid mahogany furniture and raised above the ground on pillars so that giant ants and snakes didn't get in. French windows on three sides opened onto a wrap-around veranda, with distant views over colourful, half-wild vegetation to the glistening Gulf of Guinea beyond.

All of this came as a shock to two English people in their twenties from solid working-class backgrounds, who had been children in the grey war years amid shortages and privations. Mum still remembers someone showing them an orange at school one day – just *showing* them that such a thing existed. Now, outside the window in Ghana, they could see bananas growing on trees.

Still, the house provided nothing like the shock that Nestor gave them, when he presented himself at the front door as their 'house boy.' To be clear, Nestor was a twenty-eight-year-old Nigerian with a family of his own, but the post-colonial job my father got in Ghana came with decidedly colonial perks, including the man now standing in front of them.

To give them their due, both Mum and Dad threw up their hands in horror at this arrangement and Dad marched off to school to see what could be done. Nothing, as it turned out, not unless they wanted to sack Nestor and turf him out of his two-roomed, tied house in the back garden, where he lived with his wife and two young sons.

So, Mum and Dad had a servant and eventually, when I was born a couple of years later, so did I.

For ten pounds a month (equivalent to £250 now)

Nestor cooked, washed up, cleaned the house, did the laundry and ironing, shopped in the market, and – according to Mum – made innumerable cups of tea all day long.

He let himself into my parents' bungalow at six-thirty a.m. every weekday morning, made the first cuppa of the day, swept and polished the wooden floors, and prepared breakfast. After that he made the beds, washed clothes, did any odd jobs that needed doing, and went to market. He had lunch ready for one-forty-five, when Dad's school finished for the day, and was then free until six when he cooked and served the evening meal. After washing up, he turned out the lights, said "Goodnight Madame, goodnight Sir," and locked the door behind him before going off to his own home across the garden.

Obviously, this was excruciating for my parents, who grew up in modest circumstances in post-war Derby and Cambridge. They were mortified at the very concept of 'staff,' let alone a 'boy,' but accepted that dispensing with Nestor's services would cause him hardship. Mum said she apologised at first every time she asked him to do something, but then in that insidious way that colonialism operates, my parents quickly got used to 'the way things have always been done.' Which basically meant white people being waited on hand and foot by black people, and never mind Ghanaian independence and the end of Empire.

Nestor, for his part, dismissed all their qualms. He had a licence as a domestic cook and steward, which he'd earned by working as an assistant (a "little boy") to the chief steward in a large household. He could speak three languages fluently – his own Nigerian Igbo, the local dialect of Fante, and English; he could read and write in English too. He was proud of his job and aimed to work his way up further and become a chauffeur, which would afford him a higher level of respect. Although he padded about during the day in bare feet, khaki shirt and shorts, making endless cups of tea for Madame, he maintained a worn but immaculately clean and pressed uniform which he donned to serve dinner in the evening. He might have been a servant but there was nothing servile about Nestor, who resisted every entreaty to call my parents Jean and Ken, preferring the professional distance of Madame and Sir.

He kept the bungalow spick and span, ran all the domestic arrangements, and babysat me on Saturdays when Mum and Dad went to the local sports and social club to go sailing. And, in the colonial way, and presumably as he had done with other employers, Nestor cooked the meals that he thought my English parents would want. So as the sun fell, the insects buzzed around the veranda, the cicadas clicked, and the scent from the tropical blossoms carried on the stifling night air, he presented them with hearty soups, roast dinners, pies and puddings, cooked in a simple kitchen at the back of the bungalow.

"Can't we have some local food?" Mum had said after a few weeks of this, which Nestor wasn't at all happy about. Madame would not like it. It was very spicy. Wouldn't she prefer a roast joint of meat, with vegetables, potatoes and gravy?

Madame wouldn't, because Nestor couldn't possibly have known in 1960s Ghana that this was a woman who would go on to trek in Nepal, tour China, fly around Everest and drive across Canada. She didn't look like it, and there was nothing in her background to suggest it, but Mum was game for anything.

"I'd never been anywhere until I met your father," she once said. "Then he asked me to marry him and we drove to Barcelona for our honeymoon."

"I don't need to hear about the honeymoon."

"We spent all week in bed …"

"I *really* don't need to hear about the honeymoon."

"Poisoned. *Paella* I think."

As an aside, but entirely apposite, she once asked me, when I was at college, if anyone had ever offered me drugs.

"Erm, heavens no, Mother, for I am a good boy."

"Shame," she said. "If you ever come across any marijuana, get some because I'd like to have a go."

Which is by way of saying that Nestor was obliged to go and cook something Ghanaian for the next meal and the dish he chose was groundnut soup.

The thing you need to know is that it's not really a soup – more of a blended stew made from peanuts, tomatoes, onions, ginger and red peppers, in which is cooked chicken or fish. The peanuts are the 'groundnuts,' which you can buy in any West African market, already crushed to a paste and served from a glistening, oily mound of the size and dimension that Richard Dreyfuss grappled with in his kitchen in *Close Encounters of the Third*

Kind. By red peppers, I mean chilli peppers, the more the merrier if you're Ghanaian, though I imagine Nestor played it safe the first time he served it up to my parents.

I'm not sure how a meat stew laced with eye-watering chillies is any better a bet for a sweltering, tropical meal than a roast dinner, as far as suffering from indigestion and night-sweats goes. Be that as it may, the meal was a hit and groundnut soup became a fixture in Nestor's dinner repertoire.

I was only a baby at this point and even in the 1960s, when you could still smoke in hospitals, wear asbestos trousers and drink leaded paint, it wasn't considered reasonable to feed the under-ones a stew that registered a million on the Scoville scale. Consequently, I only got to taste this dish twenty-five years later when I lived in London and stumbled one night into a part restaurant-part cultural venue called The Africa Centre, near Covent Garden.

They served a fiery Ghanaian groundnut soup, washed down with a bottle of throaty Algerian red, which is the sort of fusion meal that somehow never makes it into the Sunday supplements. I was hooked and went back for *egusi* soup, *jollof* rice, chilli-fried plantain, and several other tastes of the place I was born but didn't remember, because I was less than a year old when the folks called it quits and returned to Britain.

Forty years after that – a father myself by now, but unaccountably with no servants – I went back to Ghana with my aged parents to re-visit my roots. We took photographs in the back garden of the Takoradi bungalow where Dad had once taken a picture of Nestor holding me – a photograph that will stand on my mother's side table until she too joins Dad in the everlasting thereafter, no doubt eternally discussing the relative merits of Lidl and Morrisons.

After a few days in our old town of Takoradi, we ventured north to the former royal capital of Kumasi and stayed in an upmarket bed-and-breakfast run by Chris, an enterprising Canadian man, and his lovely Ghanaian wife, Charity. They in turn arranged for us to be given a market tour by an equally lovely local guide called Comfort, and if you ever wanted to be looked after by two nominate-determinate people it would be Charity and Comfort. Under their guidance, vast quantities of groundnut paste were purchased and that afternoon I was given a chef's toque and inducted into the mysterious preparation of groundnut soup.

Obviously, I can't reveal the exact process. If I did, then – the names were misleading – Charity and Comfort would have to hunt you down and kill you. They were very clear about that. But I can say that if you can't find any groundnut paste, in North Yorkshire or North Carolina, say, then you can substitute peanut butter, though it really wants to be the unsweetened, hand-knit, hair-shirt type. You add this to a blend of onions, root ginger, tomatoes and spices, chuck in some on-the-bone chicken and cook until the oil from the peanuts rises to the surface. If you've ever had a proper Southeast Asian *satay* sauce, then you can begin to appreciate the taste of groundnut soup, though it really isn't the same thing at all. The potential for a Ghanaian-Indonesian punch-up would be quite high if you tried to suggest it was.

Mum and Dad returned to the UK in 1963, after three years in Ghana, when I was about ten months old. The next Madame and Sir in the teachers' bungalow inherited Nestor and his roast dinners, and the Brown family returned to its servant-less ways.

But I've still got Charity's secret groundnut soup recipe scrawled on the back of a photocopied yellow fever certificate, of all things, and I make it occasionally. Stirring the soup and skimming the oil, it's possible to hear the call of the birds in the garden as Nestor – at Madame's urging – picks up the baby boy. Dad takes the picture just a fraction too soon, capturing me with a slight scowl while Nestor looks across the frame, smiling, holding his employer's child before setting him down and going off to cook dinner.

BEHIND THE SCENES IN BLACKPOOL

I'M STANDING on the seafront promenade in Blackpool, waiting for a tram. The stop is opposite a neon-lit bar, with the door guarded by a bouncer in a tight suit. The door is wedged open and, while you can't see much more than an entranceway and corridor beyond, you can hear the music pounding out a beat from somewhere inside. It's the middle of the afternoon, so there's a bit of a wait for the next tram, which means I have plenty of time to hear a couple of tunes, followed by the DJ attempting to drum up some enthusiasm from the punters for a special promotional event.

"Any ladies want to come up on the stage? Anyone?"

He plays another dance track, pleads a bit more – to no avail – and then delivers what he clearly thinks is a winning argument.

"C'mon ladies," he says, "prizes to be won if you'll come up on stage. You don't even have to get your tits out or anything."

So many questions.

Most fundamental is, I think, the unsaid suggestion that while normally you might have to get them out, on this occasion it will be acceptable if you don't.

Also, it's the middle of the afternoon, which is not, generally speaking, tits-out time. And indeed, the DJ has graciously waived the requirement. But it is the Lancashire resort of Blackpool in summer, and there are prizes to be had. The overall impression is that tits would normally have to be produced, whatever the time of day, if ladies wanted to acquire some fine promotional gifts.

I'd like to be able to say that Blackpool isn't really like this. But it is, a bit – and it's probably best to know what you're letting yourself in for, if you fancy a trip to England's most renowned seaside resort.

Later, I'm sitting on a suede sofa in a boutique hotel suite, thinking about opening the complimentary wine. It's a handsome, grown-up space – all earth tones and hardwood floors, with a Hypnos bed and a designer fire-place – and if you hadn't been to Blackpool before, you might be forgiven for thinking that this is a surprise.

Certainly, if you'd only walked the terraced back streets, past the traditional guest houses with their lace-clad windows, enterprising names – Bella Vista, Shangri-La, Royal Lodge – and enticing amenities ('colour TVs'; 'central heating'), you wouldn't be expecting any kind of boutique stylings in town. In old Edwardian Blackpool, or even cheeky Sixties' Blackpool, having a fire in your room meant a coal scuttle and a poker, not a push-button remote control. The archaic typefaces, out-dated colour schemes and weathered frontages are still thick on the ground, with a dropped 'o' from a 'Hotel' sign here and the sybaritic promise of an en-suite shower room there. This, you might think, is what Blackpool is still largely like, but you'd be wrong.

The only surprising thing about the boutique hotel I'm staying in is not its existence – there are plenty of others – but its view, which is quintessentially Blackpool. Throw open the room doors on to my Juliet balcony and I am not looking out at palm trees or roller-blading couples in Lycra but, instead, the rollercoasters in Britain's finest amusement park, Blackpool Pleasure Beach. There's loud and continuous shrieking now, but in the morning when I wake up, before the crowds start to arrive, it's a peaceful scene of latticed, contoured steel and flashes of sunlight.

There's the Pleasure Beach and there's the actual beach, and if you're not interested in either then a holiday in Blackpool is a tougher sell. But if you think you know amusement parks and sandy beaches, and dismiss them, then you haven't been to Blackpool. Fine, you're too chicken ever to ride Revolution, Avalanche, The Big One, or anything with Blast in its title, but so what? The vintage wooden rollercoasters known as 'woodies' are for the real aficionados – people come from all over the world to ride the original Big Dipper, constructed in 1923, or the 1935 Grand National, where open wooden carriages race each other on a twin track. The signs say, "Please keep your hands inside the vehicle at all times." Generations of woodie riders say, "Nah, you're all right," and wave their hands in the air through-out, as they rattle around a rollercoaster ride coming up to its first century in operation.

The beach, meanwhile, is made up of seven miles of finely sifted sand, which puts every other British seaside resort firmly in its place. At low tide, the expanse is over-whelming, the horizon infinite – a vast sand carpet for picnic-blanket families, sunburned drunks, Speedo dads, disdainful teens, languid couples and determined pensioners. There are three entertainment piers – most resorts make do with one – striding out across the sand and into the ocean, the northernmost dating back to 1863 and the central one complete with a hundred-foot-high Ferris wheel. The electric tramway, meanwhile, was first installed in 1885 and is one of the oldest such lines in the world, running all the way along the seafront between Blackpool and the fishing port of Fleetwood.

This, surely, is what Blackpool is really like? An unbroken line of brash, seaside fun, ever since the first coming of the railway in the 1840s, which disgorged passengers from the industrial cities of the north for a break away from the factories and mines. Entire counties or even countries used to descend for a week of cheerful high-jinks, as the accents of Yorkshire, Scotland and Wales flooded the so-called 'Golden Mile' along the seafront for fish and chips, donkey rides, candy floss, amusement arcades, souvenir stalls, kiss-me-quick hats and smutty postcards.

Where other resorts were genteel, Blackpool was rude and risqué. You didn't catch ukulele-strumming, music-hall star George Formby holidaying at the royal resort of Brighton, but rather strolling along the promenade here, handling his suggestive little stick of Blackpool Rock ("It's nice to have a nibble at it now and again").

Well, yes, Blackpool is still like this – and, yet again, it isn't. There's never been anything cheap about the town's attractions, which have been big and spectacularly bold from the earliest days onwards.

The old Edwardian pubs were shimmering palaces of drink, where the working man could down a pint in extravagantly decorated interiors. Yates' Wine Lodge on Talbot Square, built in 1868, had a rotunda and a stained-glass canopy, and served champagne on draft. A night on the town meant dressing up for the ornate Winter Gardens and Opera House, being entertained by stars of stage and screen – Lily Langtry and Charlie Chaplin in the early days, Nat King Cole and Frank Sinatra in the Fifties, and even the Beatles in 1964. Other events were held in the ornate Spanish Hall, a vast, staged space designed to resemble an entire Andalusian village. Dancing, meanwhile, took place in the extraordinary Tower Ballroom, with its gilded walls, painted murals and sprung wooden floor.

If you wanted a seaside view then you climbed to the top of the five-hundred-foot-high, Eiffel-like, Blackpool Tower, commissioned by earnest Victorian city elders who doubtless had taken one look at the version in Paris and thought they could do better. They could and did, by adding a permanent circus arena between the giant tower legs, which has put on a show every season since opening in 1894, even during wartime. Marvel all you like at the Parisian skyline, but you couldn't then go downstairs and see lions, tigers and elephants. In Blackpool you could, at least until 1990, when changing times saw the suspension of the animal acts.

Those buildings – and that Blackpool – are still there, part of the town's confused self-image. On one hand, stag parties carousing in the street; on the other, TV's sequinned *Strictly* dancers cavorting under the mirror ball in the Tower Ballroom, showing that Blackpool glam is still a force to be reckoned with.

Or take oysters, as a signifier of changing times. Oysters are posh and fancy. There's an oyster and champagne bar in the Pleasure Beach these days, and any number of swish bars and restaurants in town will serve you a gussied-up prawn cocktail and an oyster Kilpatrick. But go back to the time of Charles Dickens – writing at the start of Blackpool's rise – and everyone was eating oysters. They were a poor man's food, with shucked shells piled high outside humble eating houses. "It's a very remarkable circumstance, Sir," says Sam Weller in *The Pickwick Papers*, "that poverty and oysters always seem to go together."

I'm back on the promenade, looking for an old haunt, just up from the Tower, near the North Pier. Roberts' Oyster Rooms is the kind of place that every British seaside town used to have – a dainty, wood-panelled café serving oysters, cockles, mussels and prawns to the good folk of Blackpool and beyond since 1876. I first came here a century later, in the 1980s, for half a dozen oysters, a bit of bread and butter, a pot of tea, or even a pint brought in from the pub around the corner – it's the sort of place you'd want to hold on to, if you were truly bothered about the heritage. It's gone, of course, or actually, even worse – the original façade is still there, and you can still buy oysters and seafood, but only from a modern takeaway counter amid the greasy fish and chips, sticks of tooth-breaker rock and soft-serve ice cream.

On to the Imperial Hotel then, a huge, Victorian, red-brick pile overlooking the sea, with a Palm Court restaurant and plenty of old-time swagger. There's glamour of sorts here in the Number Ten bar, another of those extravagant and elegant but democratic spaces that are open to everyone in town.

For decades, Blackpool hosted annual party-political conferences of all colours, back in the days when they weren't stage-managed to death. Politicians, fixers, advisors, hacks and hustlers would all hang out at the Number Ten, spilling drinks and confidences. Prime Ministers still line the wall, with portraits of Wilson, Heath, Blair and Thatcher glaring down as you sip a botanical gin. (That's not even the strangest photo line-up in town – there's a MacDonald's on the seafront near the Central Pier with a framed picture of the time Bill Clinton and Kevin Spacey dropped by for a late-night burger.)

My friend, James, in his youth, did stints in Blackpool's kitchens and dining rooms, taking holiday jobs and short-term gigs up and down the Golden Mile. "Doing a bit," he called it, as in, "I'll be doing a bit this summer" –

which meant a spell of catering work, long hours and badly paid, in establishments with crusty old waiters, terrifying chefs and permanently hungover kitchen porters. "You'd never eat there, if you knew what went on," was a regular refrain, and then he'd regale us with stories of kitchen fights and atrocities committed upon food and customers alike.

It didn't matter how prestigious the hotel or restaurant, how upscale the experience beyond the kitchen galley doors. There was something about Blackpool – its air, its booze, its loose morals, its late-night dive-bars, and dawn-opening greasy spoons – that got under the skin of its floating army of itinerant workers and egged them on to ever greater and more appalling excess. In one small hotel – set back in the terraces, unheralded and unloved – James was schooled in the Blackpool ways of breakfast preparation. No one wanted to get up at six in the morning to cook for the punters, so the night before, the kitchen hands simply fried everything in advance, eggs included, and clingfilm-wrapped it, ready for re-heating the next day. No one, said James, ever complained.

Later, after another drink, I'm thinking about dinner. I don't want pizza or fish and chips, which once upon a time would have been disastrous, because that's all there was, but Blackpool is nothing if not adaptable. These days I could have sushi, or organic saltmarsh lamb, or tapas, or *pad Thai*, but I choose a quiet-looking place that serves Caribbean food, because I think it will be nice to have something different for a change.

I'm early and the restaurant is empty, but I'm given a

small table in the corner, out of the way, which seems a bit unreasonable until the restaurant fills suddenly with loud groups of mostly young women. The music goes up several decibels and then the waiters start to bring out the dishes, which they deliver to the tables in a fashion I've not seen before – namely, after negotiating a limbo bar while not spilling or dropping their orders.

Different is what I wanted, but – so many questions. Mostly to do with health and safety, sure, but I'm also wondering if they only pick recipes that result in gloopy food that won't slide off the plate. And do you have to have limbo experience or will they train you on the job?

As the night wears on, the limbo bar is lowered and the waiters gamely meet the challenge, as does anyone brave or unwise enough to get up from their seat. A routine visit to the bathroom involves the mass chanting of "lim-bo, lim-bo" and boos if you decline to join in. These young women are downing copious amounts of brightly coloured cocktails and are joyously over-refreshed; they are not women you would want to be booed by, or whose attention you would otherwise want to catch, so I stay put.

I'd like to be able to say that most restaurants in Blackpool aren't like this, but to be honest, it's entirely possible that they are. Other meals I have had in town have incorporated at least one table magician and a drag act. At my hotel, you can have dinner and a hot ice show, and while I don't think that's a euphemism, it still doesn't sound very relaxing.

The next morning, it's time to check out and I am on

my way down to reception in the lift. The doors open at an intermediate floor and two young men enter, smelling of stale booze and talking about their night out. There is, it seems, a question to answer – the whereabouts of one of them, at some point during the evening. He explains that he was ejected from the club and that's why his friend couldn't find him. But he is puzzled, and wonders what it was about his behaviour that resulted in the bouncer manhandling him onto the pavement. He's adamant that he did nothing wrong.

"After all," he says, "I only kissed her arse."

Blackpool. So. Many. Questions.

A WEDDING CRASHER IN SICILY

THE BUS DROPS me off by the side of the road, below the village. A couple of other people get out, look at me oddly – a stranger with a backpack – and then make their way slowly up the hill with their shopping bags.

The bus is the only way to get here and the next onward service isn't until the following morning. I hitch the pack onto my shoulders and follow the people up into the small, stone village, where white houses with red roofs bake in the heat.

Find a bar and ask the way, that's the plan.

An hour later – my bag left with a reluctant bar-owner – I'm heading along a rough path into a sheer, high-sided valley, where ancient, rock-cut tombs are hidden inside large, dome-shaped caves. In use between two and three thousand years ago, this site is as extraordinary as it is commonplace in Sicily, an island that measures its civilised history in millennia. Inspired by the great tombs of Mycenae in Greece and used for burials by a culturally rich but long-forgotten people, this was once a significant necropolis where archaeologists discovered ornate funerary ware, including a decorated gold bowl now in the British Museum.

And yet, here are the caves and tombs today – empty, echoing, largely unknown. It's just one of scores of similar sites in Sicily, whose rich, multi-cultural, multi-layered history is without compare in Europe. I negotiate the rock-cut steps and sit in silence in the double-domed cavern known as the 'Tomb of the Prince' and wonder – which prince, and when, and how did he meet his end?

I think about the practicalities of the route here and write down some notes, because this is my job. It's not always caves and tombs, but – in Sicily – it is very often sites like this, buried in the scrub and undergrowth, in the middle of nowhere. Historically significant places, archaeological sites, natural wonders and ancient buildings; things you won't necessarily know about or have even heard of, but which you might be persuaded to visit, if you read about them in a guidebook.

That's my job. To fill a book with sights, attractions and destinations and make them sound fascinating. Plenty of them write themselves – the cathedrals, beaches, markets, Byzantine mosaics, Norman churches, Greek temples and Roman amphitheatres. They don't need me to do much except expand upon their beauty or historical importance; readers know what a church or a temple looks like, all I have to do is find some suitably inspiring words.

But other entries in the guide start with an article in a

newspaper, a line in a history book or a photograph in a local tourist brochure. Abandoned hillside villages, ancient quarries, tumbledown castles, collapsed aqueducts, weathered mosaics, overgrown chapels – there's no shortage of forgotten history in Sicily. Not everything makes the cut. Some sites are just too niche, too obscure, too dull, too overgrown.

And this one? This one is all right, I think, as I close the notebook. There's a sense of mystery and grandeur here, hidden in the dry folds of a harsh Sicilian landscape. This is where generations of people buried their dead and celebrated their lives as they did so. There's enough to spark the imagination; enough to suggest that it will be worth the journey.

Mind you, it's more of a journey for me than it will be for many of my eventual readers, because on this trip I'm travelling around by public transport. This is Sicily and therefore seeking out an abandoned cave in the back of beyond, without driving, means a once-a-day bus and an overnight stop in a small village undeniably short on entertainment.

This is also my job – spending far longer than is strictly necessary in towns and villages that other, normal, people might drive through or past. I'm not, for one minute, going to suggest in the guidebook that anyone stays here for the night. I'd get letters of complaint. But I'll have to, I have no choice.

I make my way back out of the dry valley, stumbling over stones and kicking up dust, and walk into the village. I retrieve my bag and wander through the few streets to find a small guest house. It's less surprising than it sounds, that there is somewhere to stay here – there's usually a room or two, even in the smallest, most out-of-the-way place, for bus drivers, salespeople, family visitors and even, on occasion, enterprising tourists.

I hand over my passport, sign the register and head upstairs to find the room. The guest house is typically furnished – thin mattress on the bed, hard pillow, flimsy metal shower cubicle, see-through cotton towel, and throw-open shutters onto a wrought-iron balcony. There's a wooden bedside table with nothing in the drawer. No TV. You don't plan on having a big night in, staying in a Sicilian guest house.

Back outside, I explore the village. It's also typical. A couple of shops, a butcher's and a bakery, both closed, because it's four in the afternoon or Tuesday or the local saint's day or who knows, because it's Sicily. There's a barber's shop – there's always a barber's shop – and one of those mysterious Sicilian emporiums that sells vacuum cleaners, candles, oranges, sliced meat and buckets. Meanwhile, the bar features a selection of wizened old men and a range of day-old pastries, and from a metal table outside I sit and watch the village slip into an early evening torpor.

At least there will be dinner. The food is invariably good in Sicily, a highlight of the day; especially of a day like this, when my job has amounted to an hour or two spent in the dusty hills among scampering lizards.

There's only one place that's open and I walk through the door into an empty restaurant. Again, typical. I'm not particularly worried. The owner or chef will be around somewhere. I sit at a table covered with a white paper tablecloth and wait.

After five minutes or so, I get up and walk across to the counter at the back, to see if anyone's there. There isn't, but through an adjacent door I can hear the murmuring of diners and an occasional round of gentle applause. I open that door and walk through.

The wedding meal has obviously been going on for some time. There are plates and bottles on most of the tables, and people are chatting and laughing. Bride, groom and parents are sitting at a top table, formally dressed. No one notices me except a waiter, who approaches with an enquiring look.

I try a few words of Italian – Restaurant? Open? – and the waiter shakes his head and gestures at the wedding party. I nod and turn to leave, but he catches me at the door and steers me towards a small table in the corner at the back of the room. He makes a signal with his hands – "Stay there" – and disappears off to the kitchen. He's soon back with a basket of bread and cutlery and, five minutes after that, appears with a bowl of pasta.

This is unexpected. Then again, it's Sicily. Expecting things to work in an entirely normal way – restaurant closed, sign on the door saying 'Private Function' – doesn't get you very far here. It seems that the waiter has taken it upon himself to add a plus-one to the party. And chances are high that he's not really a waiter but the mayor or the chief of police, helping out for the day. Again, Sicily.

My presence is finally registering with the assembled guests, who seem positively giddy that a stranger has turned up to help them celebrate. I keep interrupting my meal to return sly waves and thumbs' up signs from across the room; small children are sent over to investigate. The pasta bowl is taken away and another course arrives, without any input from me. Then the drinks start arriving, sent over by guests, who mime toasts and salutes as I start to work my way through a line of glasses set out in front of me.

At some point later, the atmosphere changes. Silence falls as a young man stands up and starts to sing. It appears to be a traditional song, operatic in its intensity, which he belts out unaccompanied, with occasional grand gestures. His voice rises and falls, the song finishes and the room erupts. There's wild cheering and clapping, amid which another person is encouraged to their feet and a new song starts. This one is similar in style, if a little less flamboyant, and the audience joins in with well-known words at a repeated chorus. By now, I'm on my third or fourth drink. I smile across the room, tapping along on the table, sipping from yet another glass.

There are more songs, more cheering, more drinks. And then a man gets up from the wedding party, with everyone deep in conversation, and makes his way over to my table. He welcomes me in halting English and asks where I'm from.

England, I tell him. This is a lovely party. Thank you.

He says something else, and at first I don't understand. Then he has another go, phrasing the sentence in a slightly different way.

A song please. From your country.

He looks behind him, to the wedding party, where people are now taking an interest in our conversation, and gestures to the place in front of the tables where the previous singers have stood.

I pretend I don't understand, to buy some time, because this is clearly a terrible idea. I don't sing, I don't know any songs, and I definitely don't sing songs I don't know in public in front of a wedding party.

He smiles encouragingly. A song please. From your country.

I tap my temple with my finger, as if I'm thinking, to try and buy some more time. There are sharp intakes of breath, as an entire Sicilian wedding party watches me indicate to the man that I think he's mad. He looks mortally offended, so I smile widely and try the medium of mime to express that, while that's a very kind offer and it's very generous of them to include me in their party, I'm not sure that any song I could muster would be in keeping with the quality already displayed.

The medium of mime, it's fair to say, isn't really up to the job in hand. In any case, by now it's far too late for further prevarication, because assorted Sicilian brothers, sisters, uncles, aunts, cousins and grandparents are clapping in unison at an increasing tempo and the man is pulling me to my feet.

I stand in front of the tables and think desperately. I

have maybe ten or fifteen seconds before an awkward silence starts. Right now, I'm being given a huge benefit of the doubt. I need a song of more than one verse that I know the words to, and it really needs to be a traditional tune rather than, say, the Sex Pistols' 'Anarchy in the UK', which is the only song to which I know all the words that is currently lodged in my wine-addled brain. Even with the language barrier firmly in place, I'm not sure that serenading a Sicilian wedding party with the words "I am an antichrist, I am an anarchist" will be entirely suitable.

I reach into the depths of my school-assembly-Scout-campfire childhood and suddenly find myself singing, surprisingly strongly:

"Wheear 'ast tha bin sin' ah saw thee, ah saw thee?

On Ilkley Moor baht 'at."

The Yorkshire dialect is often impenetrable to other English speakers; rather like Sicilian to Italians, in fact. For this reason, I'm largely unconcerned that the bride and groom will be wondering why I'm asking, "Where have you been since I last saw you?" and answering, "On Ilkley Moor, without a hat."

I'm more interested in getting through the ordeal with my dignity intact and to that extent my subconscious seems to have picked a winner. The tune is a rollicking, oompah-style round, with a repeated chorus of "On Ilkley Moor baht 'at," that even a half-sozzled Sicilian wedding party can grasp. Encouraged by their full-throated participation, I give the other verses a go, not worrying too much about the content, which is possibly even less suited to a wedding than 'Anarchy in the UK.'

Basically, the 'you' in the song has unwisely been on a windswept, rain-sodden Yorkshire moor without a hat (the meaning of 'baht 'at'), while courting a local lass, name of Mary Jane. If you know anything about York-shire moors – you'll have read *Wuthering Heights*, for example – you'll know that's a cavalier thing to have done. Hats are essential, when it comes to the heather-clad wastes of Yorkshire. Having been on Ilkley Moor without one, you consequently catch your death of cold, are buried and eaten by worms, which in turn are eaten by ducks, which we then all eat, so that ultimately, we have all "etten thee." The general Yorkshire consensus of opinion is that you've only got yourself to blame. Going moorland courting without a hat, what were you thinking?

I am, though I say it myself, going down a storm. There is cheering as I start the song, cheering through-out, and a bring-the-house-down roar as I finish with a flourish. I sit down triumphant, now invited to a closer table, and more drinks are lined up before me. I leave some hours later, with lots of new friends and no sugges-tion of a bill for anything that I've eaten or drunk.

When people ask me what I do for a living, I say 'travel writer' and mostly go along with the assumptions that go with that. Yes, I get to travel the world and write about it. But I also know that no one ever imagines that might mean singing a cannibalistic Yorkshire dialect song about worms and ducks to two people about to embark on the next chapter of their lives.

Travel, that's just one part of it. Sometimes, getting off a bus in the middle of nowhere, scratching about in a dusty cave and singing for my supper is my job too.

ON THE OUTLANDER TRAIL IN SCOTLAND

"It's my birthday soon," says Elaine, about three months before her actual birthday, because she has very particular requirements. For a start, the idea that this is just a single day of celebration is laughable. Often, she refers to her 'birthday week' or 'birthday month' just so I get the message. I'm not entirely sure that, in Elaine's mind, her next birthday doesn't start on the day immediately after the last one.

Buying a gift is not even the half of it, I can tell you from experience.

"That's a lovely diamond-encrusted necklace," she might say, had I ever bought such a thing (and, indeed, were she the type of person who would want such a thing, which she isn't). But it would be said in a tone that suggests disappointment that you have failed to have the necklace delivered by unicorn as the highpoint of a week's festivities ordered by royal decree.

And if you buckle under the pressure and simply ask

what she wants for her birthday, then the gist of her advice is, "Go big or go home, buster."

This is by way of setting the scene for this year's celebration, about which, for once, I'm reasonably confident. She is going to love what I have planned, spanning as it does multiple days and experiences. It's not a gift *per se*, but a sensory travel immersion, tailor made for the special person in my life. All right, it's a surprise holiday to Scotland, but I guarantee its success, for it is devoted entirely to one of the things that Elaine loves most in the world, namely the *Outlander* TV series.

I'll assume you're familiar with this programme. If not, it's basically a time-travel history romp with big frocks, tartan kilts and massive dirks (be careful how you Google that last one). Adapted from a series of novels by Diana Gabaldon – who, famously, had never been to Scotland before she started writing them – it's the story of a World War II army nurse who finds herself mysteriously transported back to 1743 and gets caught up in the Jacobite rebellion. If that doesn't sound like your kind of thing, I urge you to persevere with an episode or two, for there are untold charms to come.

We don't binge-watch, it's fair to say, for the historical verisimilitude, though the novels are scrupulously researched and the TV series is a magnificently staged period drama. For my part, I'm not entirely sure what it is about *Outlander* that appeals – it's either the stupendous Scottish locations or the clothing-optional, five-foot-ten, former model and actress Caitríona Balfe, who plays the time-travelling nurse, Claire Randall. She falls in with a group of Highland rebels and marries one of them, Jamie Fraser, played by six-foot-two Scottish actor Sam Heughan. When casting Jamie, the recipe clearly called for one part beef and one part cake. When he takes his shirt off, which is often, and flexes his stomach muscles – also, regularly, for no apparent plot-related reason – it's as if a fleet of ferrets is chasing up and down underneath his skin, such is the rippling and bulging.

"Pass the salt," Claire will say, as they sit down to a meal of neeps and tatties, or some similar Highland delicacy.

"Aye lass," Jamie will growl, "though the fire is high this evening and I find myself too warm for comfort. Help me off with this, will ye?"

I often catch Elaine staring dreamily at the Scottish scenery, wondering when it's going to remove its billowy shirt again – or, as on several memorable occasions, its 'breeks'.

Consequently, a surprise tour of the Scottish filming locations in *Outlander* is very much in the category of Excellent Birthday Presents. It may indeed be my all-time winner, but there is a flaw in my cunning travel plan.

The 'surprise' part of the surprise trip is going well so far, in that Elaine has no idea where we're going or why, but shortly I'm going to be in the same clueless position, as – to maintain the mystery – I've had to hide the SatNav. We're fast running out of English towns that we could be going to, but aren't, and sooner or later I'm going to have to narrow 'Scotland' down a bit if we're to hit our first mystery destination.

I consider stopping in a layby and blindfolding her, but to be fair to Elaine she's quite broadminded and might jump to the wrong conclusion about what sort of surprise trip this really is. Also, I suspect there's a strong possibility that if you drive along the M74 for long enough with a blindfolded woman in the passenger seat, you run the risk of a motorway chase, armed intervention and an appearance on the evening news.

I needn't have worried, because I had forgotten about Elaine's one saving characteristic on occasions such as this, namely the fact that she's Irish. She may have lived in the UK for many years, but even so there's a certain sketchiness to her geographical knowledge that was just about to come to my aid. I know, I couldn't point out Tralee on a map, or tell you the difference between Wexford and Wicklow, but that is very much not the point here.

"Is it Cornwall?" she says, as we sail past Carlisle.

"Ooh, I know, the Cotswolds," as Lockerbie recedes into the distance.

Eventually, as all the signs start to say 'Edinburgh,' I switch the SatNav back on, smile knowingly and refuse to answer any more questions. It turns out that you can get away with "Edinburgh" as the unsaid answer to "Where are we going?" for ages, as most of the *Outlander* locations are all in the same general area, close to Edinburgh on either side of the Firth of Forth estuary. And Edinburgh would be firmly in Birthday Surprise territory in any case, so I let her continue thinking that we're bound for the Scottish capital until we drive up a track, off a country road near Queensferry. Even Elaine recognises that this is not the fair seat of Scotland's government.

"This doesn't look like there's going to be a boutique hotel here," she says, accurately and accusingly.

She still doesn't know where we are until I park the car and lead her around the corner, to stand in front of the arched gateway to sixteenth-century Midhope Castle, a tall, bulky, stone tower-house with sheer walls and a steeply pitched roof. If you know *Outlander*, you'd know it immediately, and so does Elaine, who squeals with delight. Literally squeals.

"Lallybroch!"

Jamie Fraser's ancestral home features intermittently in the first three seasons, but it's an iconic location, full of the promise of home and family for many of the *Outlander* characters. You have to pay – quite a lot – for parking and you can't go inside the building, but even so, we spend a happy half-hour wandering around the court-yard, posing on the steps and gazing up at the high windows, while at my request Elaine softly warbles "Lally-broch" in a Caitríona-Balfe-like manner.

She also pulls her coat and scarf close – it's a freezing cold day – and wishes that she had just a fraction of the wardrobe that La Balfe routinely displays while flouncing around the Scottish countryside. There's an entire sub-set of *Outlander* fans that watch the show for the costumery alone – the shawls, wraps, kilts, cloaks and dresses – and Elaine is firmly in that bracket, albeit in the sub-sub-set that also enjoys a breek-less Highlander.

Clan-rebel Jamie's shirt is, as we know, rarely on,

which unfortunately makes him susceptible to all sorts of unpleasantness inflicted by the heinous English Redcoats. Or "Your lot," as they are known in our household.

Our lot are indeed reprehensible, variously oppressing the Highland clans, kicking the peasantry off their land, and butchering the Jacobites at Culloden. Both actual history and TV history are clear about the misery caused by the English in their colonial ravages. It's a wonder they let us into Scotland at all these days, or indeed that Elaine – daughter of Éirinn – puts up with me. Jamie Fraser's bare back, meanwhile, is like a red rag to a bull in the shape of *Outlander*'s villainous Redcoat, 'Black Jack' Randall, who not only attacks Claire at every opportunity but is also an unlikely ancestor of Claire's 1943 husband, Frank, both of whom – Black Jack and Frank – are played by the same actor, Tobias Menzies.

Keep up. There will be a quiz later.

Anyway, poor Jamie, as we come to think of him, gets flogged at Lallybroch quite early on in the proceedings, so we try not to think about that as we leave the courtyard and return to the car. But there's much worse to come for him at my next secret surprise stop, which is nearby Blackness Castle, perched on a promontory on the south side of the Forth estuary.

"Fort William?" shudders Elaine, as we park outside, referring to the name it's given in the series, where it stands in as the English army's castle and prison.

"I'm afraid so."

"Poor Jamie," she says, which I'd say pretty much covers the brutal beating, torture and assault upon his person in the castle by equal-opportunity rapist 'Black Jack' Randall.

It's a grim site in any case, a forbidding fifteenth-century coastal fortress, lapped by the tides and known because of its shape as the 'ship that never sailed.' We walk the grey walls as the wind whips across the water, while Elaine – using poor Jamie as a starting-point – enumerates the many and varied ways that "Your lot" have oppressed the Celtic peoples of the British Isles, of which she has a full and in-depth knowledge.

"It isn't actually my fault," I say. "It was three hundred years ago."

"I'm not so sure," she says.

We drive an hour west, to the fringes of the Loch Lomond and The Trossachs National Park, where I have booked a hotel for the night. It's not a success on its own terms, though it would be a contender in the hotly contested award categories, World's Coldest Room and World's Smallest Breakfast. The breakfast is beguilingly begrudging, featuring one small fried egg, one thin sausage and, my favourite item, literally one mushroom. Someone has had to think about this breakfast; this is food with something to say; this is a fried insult.

"This is my fault," I say. "This, I can be blamed for. The Highland clearances, not so much."

Nonetheless, I am upbeat and Elaine is still, just about, on side with things, because she has by now worked out that there is more *Outlander*-related jollity to come today. And twenty minutes' drive down the road, back towards Stirling, I elicit more squealing when I pull into the car park at Doune Castle – or Castle Leoch, the seat of *Outlander*'s Clan MacKenzie, used many times in filming.

Unlike Midhope, it's a proper medieval castle with royal connections – foursquare and fortified, with a huge courtyard, soaring great hall and cavernous kitchens. Dating from the fourteenth century, it was the seat of Robert Stewart, an eminent duke who was the uncrowned but effective king of Scotland from the 1380s until 1420.

They lived well here, you can tell from the grand proportions and cathedral-like spaces. Narrow, winding, stone staircases run up and down to hidden chambers with arrow-slit windows, and we bustle in and out of ornate, echoing rooms, though not for long, as the place soon fills up with coach parties. It's not just the *Outlander* connections people come for – Doune was first used as a set in *Monty Python and the Holy Grail*, so before you leave you'll definitely want to go up to the top and shout, "I fart in your general direction, your mother was a hamster and your father smelt of elderberries."

The next stop is the preserved eighteenth-century village of Culross, on the north side of the Forth, with its ochre-coloured palace, whitewashed houses, cobbled streets and ancient market cross. Called Cranesmuir in the TV series, it features heavily in various storylines, but even without *Outlander*, this is a beautiful place to visit. Once a thriving river port, it's a hugely charming place of hidden gardens, period buildings, cafés and galleries. We follow a high path around the top of the village and look down over weathered rooftops and enclosed yards to the water beyond.

Later, after a drive around the Fife coastal town of Kirkcaldy, we descend to the deep cleft of Dysart Harbour, as the sun sinks lower in a glowing autumn sky. This old trading harbour doubled as Le Havre in France, when the *Outlander* story first leaves Scotland, and we walk under high, stone harbour walls, looking down onto mud-bound boats at low tide.

And so to the second overnight stop, where I think I am on much firmer ground regarding the quality of our accommodation. Falkland is another one of those lovingly preserved old stone towns, with a royal palace that was once a country hunting estate – it's surrounded by encroaching hills still alive with deer. The *Outlander* team dressed the town up as 1940s Inverness and it plays a pivotal role right at the start of the story, not least when Claire and her husband Frank stay overnight in 'Mrs Baird's Bed and Breakfast' on their post-war second honeymoon.

Or the Covenanter Hotel, as it actually is, and where I have booked a room for the night.

"Here, really?" says Elaine, almost combusting with excitement. "We're staying here? In Mrs Baird's?"

I can see that I have done well. My Englishness has never seemed less important. I'm not saying that I shall be forgiven for personally oppressing the Celtic nations, but at this stage I am so many points in credit that I may never have to buy another birthday present in my life.

The hotel will tell you that only the exterior was used

for filming – it's instantly recognisable – but that is on a strictly need-to-know basis, as far as Elaine is concerned. From our window, we look down on a familiar market square and ornate memorial fountain, and dare to dream that we have the very room in which Caitríona Balfe and Tobias Menzies got all hot and bothered and … no, it's too much for our sensibilities. We eat homemade pie in the restaurant and retire early, with one more long day ahead of us before leaving Scotland and *Outlander* behind.

Of all the locations, isolated Tibbermore Church – scene of a gripping witch-trial – is probably the most atmospheric. We drive up there the next morning, and find it on a country road, a few miles west of Perth, set back behind a low-walled graveyard. A display inside acknowledges why you've really come to see the church – Caitríona Balfe, clothes on for a change, pleading for her life! – but you get the impression they'd rather you were here to marvel at the raked box-seating, original wooden panelling, and carved, elevated pulpit. Certainly, the church website makes no mention of its connection with *Outlander*, which is quietly heroic, given that I'm sure no one drives all the way here to appreciate the "muscular style of the horseshoe seating."

There's one last destination, but it's under wraps as we head further north into the Highlands, largely because I'm not confident of finding it. Partly, this is because it's pure scenery – it's not like there's a sign or a building to locate – and partly because it doesn't really exist.

Craigh na Dun is the most iconic *Outlander* location of all. It's the MacGuffin that keeps events in motion, the plot device that explains the very concept, namely a lonely, hilltop stone circle that sends our World War II nurse back in time in the first place – and acts as an anchor for the whole story. Except that on Rannoch Moor, where filming took place, there isn't a stone circle – they brought in fake rocks, modelled on the famous Calanais stones on the Isle of Lewis in the Outer Hebrides.

However, there is an identifiable hilltop location, if only I can find it with the help of a couple of fan blogs and a page on Google maps that keeps disappearing because of the hopeless signal.

I take stock in a country café attached to a shop emblazoned with the four words no man ever wants to see: Fabrics, Yarns, Sewing Machines. I could pretend that this was our destination all along, as Elaine leaps from the car and within minutes is lost to all reason, as fabrics, yarns and sewing machines are second, third and fourth on her list of favourite things after *Outlander*. Poor Jamie, were he to appear right now, minus shirt *and* breeks, wouldn't get a second look from the assorted women inside, knee-deep as they are in yak yarn and overlockers, and fighting over limited-edition Japanese shawl patterns.

I cattle-prod her out with the promise of true romance, if only she'll trust me, though Elaine points out that, historically, simple Irish country girls such as herself have never really done well by trusting sweet-talking Englishmen.

"Dinna fash yersel," I say, borrowing one of Jamie's

most used phrases. It basically means "Don't worry yourself about it," though it tends to be rather airily employed by him, as if there isn't a care in the world, when they're just about to be flogged to death, bound in chains or any other number of terrible fates, which they then generally escape with a second to spare.

We drive further into the wilds, climbing on a high, moorland road heading towards Kinloch Rannoch. For the first time on our tour, this is more the sort of typical Scottish Highland country you might expect from a story about the rebellious clans – not yet mountainous and rugged, it's true, but windswept, wooded and pastoral, with swirling clouds over rounded hill-tops and big-sky views from the lonely road.

At a farm gate by the side of the road, a track leads up through a field to a hilltop grove of trees that we've seen many times before, sitting on our sofa at home. We stroll under a canopy of leaves, the trees neatly forming their own circle, and look down over the distant waters of a shining loch. It's Craigh na Dun all right, and we don't need the standing stones to transport us back to 1743 – there's a magic here that works for us, even if it is only a confected scene from a made-up story about a romance that spans centuries.

A rough Highlander he may be, but Jamie Fraser has a soul which is Claire's and Claire's alone.

"Blood of my blood," he says, "My life is yours … I would lay the world at your feet," and then he pulls her close and calls her "Sassenach" – a derogatory term for an English person – which is rarely used in Scotland as an endearment but is said in *Outlander* with love.

If it hasn't been clear until this point, I would do all of those things for Elaine too. She is my North, my South, my East and West, the blood of my blood, and my world besides. I can't call an Irish woman *Sassenach* – harsh words would ensue – but I do have one final gift, courtesy of some frantic wiki-translation in the hotel the night before.

I pull Elaine close as we take one last look at Craigh na Dun.

"Happy birthday *Éireannach*," I say, and we turn and walk back into the twenty-first century, leaving the magic time portal behind for the next pair of eternal souls.

LIVING THE DREAM IN PORTUGAL

HERE'S what happens when you are living the dream in a tiny hamlet in the forested hills of central Portugal.

The twinkly old gent who comes to prune his olive trees in the plot next to yours stops one day to drop off a bag of tomatoes and curly lettuce from his vegetable plot. He doesn't speak any English, but you've lived here long enough – five or six years – to be able to pass the time of day in Portuguese, ask after his family, and see if he wants a hand with reaching the higher branches. Later that day, you do a bit more work on the roof of the old barn that's part of your property, which you're turning into an office space. Your other neighbour drops by, offers a bit of advice and passes up a tool or two, before disappearing into his own house and coming back with a jug of his homemade wine. You sit out on the terrace in the shade discussing Portuguese football, and he invites you over to dinner that night because he has more fresh-tasting produce coming out of his garden than he knows what to do with.

Yeah, right.

You've clearly been reading too many Peter Mayle and Chris Stewart books. Or I just didn't do it correctly. Very possibly the latter, seeing as my experience of living in rural Portugal was less one of charming interactions and comedic misunderstandings and more in the way of an ongoing Kafka-esque entanglement. The only thing missing was the giant cockroach. No wait, I had one of those too, hiding under the cupboards in the kitchen.

Take the twinkly old gent. No, please, as the music-hall comedians used to say about their wives, take him. He thought we were ridiculous, and not just because we were English, though he did have a point there. We paid what turned out to be an insane amount for a Portuguese village house – see being English, above – which meant that every interaction with him was viewed through that prism. He owned the small olive grove right next to our house, which had been for sale for ever, and when we asked a Portuguese person – our estate agent, say, or the solicitor we used for the house – how much we should pay for it, they said a few hundred euros, seeing as how there are millions of acres of unwanted land in rural Portugal.

The twinkly gent though – actually, mean old glowering gent – wouldn't shift from ten thousand euros, even though literally no one else in the world other than me would ever be interested in that plot of land. And when he got tired of pruning the trees, and when we wouldn't meet the price, he simply came one day with a chainsaw and lopped them all off at the base and we cried.

Our actual neighbours were lovely, though they also thought we were ridiculous for paying so much for the house. I can stop saying that now – let's just work on the basis that everyone within a hundred miles thought that.

But in five years, and entirely in opposition to the Mayle-Stewart cheery neighbour hypothesis, I never set foot inside our neighbours' house or they in ours. We tried – invitations to children's birthday parties, garden drinks and barbecues; I even dropped off some home-made mince pies at Christmas one year, which they simply didn't understand at all.

The neighbours were not unfriendly. They stopped and chatted briefly in the street, asked about the children, and smiled when they saw us in the garden. They didn't disturb us in any way at all, but they didn't deliver surplus food, invite us around, offer advice or anything else that we'd been led to expect by even a cursory reading of every new-life-abroad book ever written.

They were not even the sort of awful or stand-offish neighbours you might have anecdotes about; the villagers who end up as supporting characters in the living-the-dream books. I do have a story about them, though, and it's fully in keeping with the general tenor of life in my Portuguese village.

Their garden adjoined ours at the back. Both plots started out flat and then dropped steeply to an overgrown stream at the bottom of the valley. My neighbour's side was beautifully tended, with raked and watered rows of seasonally changing produce, from cabbage to tomatoes, cherries to olives, and everything in between. He was out at every opportunity, morning and evening, weeding, planting and harvesting. I should think they never had to buy fruit or vegetables.

My side, on the other hand, was a nightmare of brambles, invasive plants, stones, and mysterious and off-putting slithering noises. I went down there now and again, thrashed about with a strimmer and made the tiniest of headways into a plot of land that I really ought to have done something about, only it was too hard and too much effort.

In a fit of early spring enthusiasm one year, I knocked together a boarded-out compost area – using tools and everything, like a real man – and started chucking the kitchen peelings in there for about ten minutes, until that also got too hard, given that it was a full five-minute walk from back door to compost heap.

My neighbour spotted me at work on the construction and asked me what I was doing, which was a rare, unprompted social interaction. I didn't have the Portuguese words for explaining exactly what it was, but did my best and figured that, as a gardener, he'd work it out.

"You can put anything in it?" he asked.

"Nothing cooked," I said. "But, you know, all the kitchen waste, things like that."

"Plastic bags?" he said, and I thought he was joking, but he was entirely serious because getting rid of plastic bags was his other main hobby. He burned them at the top of his garden at least two or three times a week, sending a pall of black, microplastic filth across the valley. And I had now introduced him to a new method of recycling, which he was very interested in.

In fact, plastic-bag ash wasn't the only additive he used in his garden. Again, primed by the Mayles and Stewarts of this world, I'd always imagined that the local produce would be organically tended in a traditional, age-old manner. The stuff available at the market always looked the part – huge, knobbly-shaped fruit and veg that spoke of the careful application of natural ingredients and arcane know-how. Well, my neighbour had literally never even heard of a compost heap before I made one, and he napalmed his back garden regularly with a liquid that came with a big red cross marked on the container. They were all at it, even the little old grannies who ran the market stalls, which is why their tomatoes were so big and radioactively red.

The grannies, by the way, were not daft. You'd stop by a stall of glowing courgettes or irradiated peppers and say, "I'd like two please," and they would indicate for you to open your shopping bag. Then before you knew what was happening, they'd tip in as many as they possibly could and name some random price, and you'd go back home with piles of unwanted produce. If you did remonstrate, they'd suddenly become deaf or claim that you said two kilos: either way, it was courgette surprise again for dinner for a week or two.

The non-twinkly gent came back another time and was spotted at the edge of our property with a spade and a small, potted orange tree. In any other book about living abroad, this is a cue for a thoughtful gift, isn't it?

Our short driveway led to a patch of open ground and a dirt track that was the only way out of the village from our house.

"It's customary, communal land," said the solicitor. "You have access across it, as do the neighbours to get to their plots."

"It's my family land," said the non-twinkly gent, who proceeded to dig a hole and plant an orange tree, which made backing the car out a fifty-point-turn manoeuvre even before the tree started to grow.

"And I might put a fence up," he said. "Do you still want the olive grove? It's ten thousand euros."

Our house was a hodgepodge of restored, connecting buildings around a small yard, with an elevated terrace that looked down over a forested valley. It was a real sun trap for most of the year, and while the view was ostensibly a monotone of plantation pine and eucalyptus trees, there was a shifting palette of green under bright, blue skies that made the heart sing when you came out with your morning coffee or sat there at dusk with a glass of wine.

But the truth was that, for different reasons, the house wasn't what either of us wanted – not enough of a fixer-upper for one, not enough of a finished house for the other, and ultimately not really in the right place for either of us.

This was not the Portugal of holiday brochures, of sun and sea, of Lisbon and the Algarve. Central Portugal has a rougher, tougher edge – hardscrabble stone villages in the hills, wildfires that burn each spring and summer, and a population that's only a generation or two out of the fields.

Hamlets like ours were mostly abandoned, as young people and families had moved to the towns – out of fifteen houses or so, only four were permanently inhabited, with the rest either left empty or used as holiday homes. And not the sort of places you see on Instagram – there wasn't a swimming pool, shade sail or hammock to be seen. These were un-lovely houses, with stainless steel doors, mildewed ceilings and brutally tiled rooms, that extended families used a few times a year to come and chop firewood, tend to their vines and pick their olives. The single alley was dusty and weed-grown, and when it rained heavily, water coursed down and pooled against cracked and rotten doors.

Our house at least had been renovated – by previous English owners, hence the high price – and was heated and double-glazed. It had that alluring quality, 'potential' – a separate guest wing, an old, attached barn, and an adjoining tumbledown cottage. But what it really needed was two people with commitment and at least one of them to know what they were doing, and it had neither.

I could put up a shelf and that was about it, which meant that when anything went wrong or broke I had to rely on a local tradesperson to come and fix it. None of them filled you full of confidence. The first plumber we ever called arrived on a moped and carried the entire tools of his trade – a couple of spanners and a hammer –

in a plastic bag. He banged everything experimentally a few times, declared himself satisfied, and left without requiring any payment – which was fair enough because naturally he hadn't fixed anything at all.

The builders we used over a couple of years had no comedy value whatsoever, despite the evidence in every tales-of-an-expat book. They were, in fact, reassuringly traditional, in that they never turned up when they said they would, promised to do things they never delivered, and knocked off early on any day ending in the word 'day.' Whatever time they actually did arrive, they then decamped almost immediately at noon to the nearest restaurant, a couple of miles down the road, and ripped through a bottle of homemade wine each alongside their meal. I know, because I was often down there too, but whereas I walked to the restaurant because I was planning on ripping through my own bottle of wine, they careered down and back in their pick-up, and then spent a woozy afternoon clambering all over the scaffolding in the blazing sun.

While the house failed to transform itself, we at least made friends, who were all English-speaking foreigners like ourselves. This was also surprising to me, because one of the attractions of central Portugal was that it billed itself as more like the 'real Portugal.' It wasn't a region of retired British expats living easy lives in the sun; I didn't think there would be too many people like us around.

Except there were – scores, if not hundreds of them, dotted around the hills and valleys living in similar hamlets and rural outposts. Granted, they weren't retired British expats, but instead tended towards the festival-going, campervan-dwelling, dog-on-a-rope end of the spectrum, attracted here by the cheap land and property. I know, how we laughed. Some didn't have houses at all, just a plot of land on which they were semi-permanently camping. The ones that did have houses didn't all have roofs or running water.

After a year or two, I genuinely knew more jugglers and *reiki* healers than I did local Portuguese people, which – don't get me wrong – was entirely my fault.

Portuguese is a hard language to learn, and though I tried I never got beyond a very basic level of comprehension. All right on restaurant menus and conversations in the present tense about the weather; completely lost the minute someone asked me an unscripted, conditional question about buying olive trees for an excessive price. The pronunciation is challenging for an English-speaker – the letter 'x' can be pronounced at least three different ways, so that the word *puxe*, for example, is actually pronounced 'pu-sh'. And all you really need to know about the difficulty of understanding Portuguese is that *puxe* ('pu-sh') means 'pull.'

It was this lack of language, for certain, that meant we never got to know our neighbours. They didn't speak English and found it embarrassing to talk to us, as our conversations went nowhere. I'd have been embarrassed to talk to people like me, who just swanned around expecting people to speak English. We didn't try hard enough, and it was far easier to make friends with a dreadlocked, part-time festival roadie-cum-tree surgeon who was ostensibly building a wooden hot-tub retreat in the hills but basically drank beer and smoked weed for a living.

I liked most of these people, and they were fun to be around – no idea what they thought about us – but we were not exactly being assimilated into the local culture. Or rather we were, just the wrong culture.

We had an excuse though. We had young children.

In retrospect, moving to a foreign country with two tiny children, no language skills and no support network was a guaranteed marriage stress-tester. (It failed the stress-test, by the way.) It was *hard*, and no amount of daily sun, cheap wine and beautiful views could mask quite how hard it became. But in time, the kids went to the neighbouring village nursery and school, where it turned out that every other foreigner also sent their children, so we started to make friends with people who could speak the same language as us.

The children grew up reading and writing Portuguese, which was extremely useful. I didn't think of taking them round to the neighbours to help, but I would be lying if I said I had never brought along a six-year-old to discuss the finer points of a garage bill with the mechanic.

Alongside their other school subjects they were set English homework, which seemed both hilarious and easy until the point at which the teacher started saying that their written answers – overseen by me – were wrong.

"You know I'm a writer" I'd say. "And English."

"I know Daddy, but it's wrong," and I'd have to change it to read grammatically incorrectly so they could get the top marks.

The school, in the end, did give us a community, though not the one we had imagined when we first moved. It gave us a routine too – a school run, plus trips, birthday parties and outings. In summer, the class would trail down to the local river in their sun hats and splash about in the water, and you could go with them, buy a cold beer from the river-beach bar, and proudly watch your children speaking another language confidently and fluently. In winter, you got roped into the big Christmas production, which culminated in the kids being given gifts on stage by Father Christmas, or *Pai Natal* as he's known in Portugal.

"It's your turn," said one of the other British dads. "They always make one of the foreigners be *Pai Natal*. And I'm not doing it again," and he shuddered.

I donned the red suit, beard and hat and waited in the wings, while they formed the children into a line on stage. I wasn't looking forward to this, on account of not really speaking Portuguese. I thought I'd get away with "Ho, ho, ho," but everything else was going to be tricky, given that ninety percent of the children in the line were expecting to have a lovely chat in Portuguese with Santa about whether they'd been naughty or nice. "The weather is fine today, it is sunny," wasn't going to cut it.

I needn't have worried, as it never got that far. The hall started to fall silent, as the children shuffled forward across the stage. My job was to stroll out to meet them, presumably to cheers. I could hear the kids talking, and even in Portuguese I could understand the excitement.

"It's *Pai Natal*!"

"*Pai Natal* is here!"

However, I could also hear dissenting voices.

"No, he's not."

"It's not *Pai Natal*."

"It is! Look!"

"No, it isn't."

The dissenting voices were my own children, who could smell a rat.

"Look, there! That's *Pai Natal*."

"No," shouted one of them. "That's not *Pai Natal*, it's my dad."

"Daddy!" said the other one.

"Ho, ho, ho," I said, emerging onto the stage.

"You're not *Pai Natal*," said one kid after another, "you're their dad. Where's *Pai Natal*?"

It was a total shambles – "Better than last year," said the other British dad, "much more entertaining" – which only really resolved itself once everyone had a present and I could slink away in shame. If there are scarred generations in central Portugal who have never really believed in the existence of *Pai Natal*, I can only apologise.

Obviously, I'm compacting the experiences and drawing simple conclusions from a few years' spent living in central Portugal. There was much to recommend our new life in the sun – not least the sun, which shone warmly and reliably from February to November. The children spent their early years in a safe, rural environment, and learned a new language which might stand them in good stead one day should they ever find themselves in Brazil or Angola. (Although maybe not, seeing as when I asked the other day what they could still remember, the only words they could come up with ten years later were *baleia* (whale) and *trator* (tractor). And if you ever find yourself in a situation requiring those exact words, it's probably already too late for the whale.)

We met some nice people and had some good times, but what we didn't do was live the dream as advertised in the Mayle-Stewart prospectus. And the lesson here is that if you plan on pursuing the dream, you should probably make sure at the outset that you both have the same dream. That would have helped.

Plus, cover your eyes my sons, small children just make things harder, wherever you choose to live. That's partly a convenient excuse for why we abandoned our experiment in 'Good Life' living, but also partly the truth, as anyone will know who has ever had to drive to the hospital casualty department with a shrieking child while looking up the Portuguese for 'head wound', 'stitches' and 'oh God, the blood, will you just look at the blood.'

That's what happens, by the way, when you live in a tiny hamlet in the forested hills of central Portugal, with building materials dropped all over the courtyard from on high.

WATCH OUT FOR PIRATES

ON THE BIRTH certificate of Stan Laurel – long before he ever met Hardy – his father's occupation was listed as 'Comedian.'

Actress and singer Liza Minnelli's mum? Actress and singer Judy Garland. Acclaimed novelist Martin Amis' dad? Acclaimed novelist Kingsley Amis. Or what about Jaden Smith, Ziggy Marley, Julian Lennon, Joe Hill, Kim Wilde, Enrique Iglesias, Dakota Johnson and Jamie Lee Curtis? All got a head start from their parentage and probably never considered doing anything else. My father travelled the world and though I'm British I was born in West Africa. What else was I going to do but travel for a living?

Travel was baked into my background. You could say it was in the family. Before me came my father, the man who cycled to France as a teenager in the 1940s, drove to Barcelona for his honeymoon in the 1950s, fathered a son in West Africa in the 1960s, and subsequently worked in forty-seven different countries, from Sweden to the Solomon Islands. He was a real traveller, though travel for Dad was a by-product of his work as a teacher and educationalist.

I grew up used to the idea of 'abroad', even living in Huddersfield in northern England (which, I appreciate, is 'abroad' to some of you, especially those from the south of England). Dad brought back weird stuff and colourful stamps from faraway places, and he invited home his students, who came not from Manchester and Cardiff but Malawi and China. There were ornaments on our mantelpiece from Nigeria and pictures of Ghana on the walls, and I had an authentic Australian boomerang that I definitely wasn't allowed to hurl around the garden for fear of braining the cat (I was trying my best to brain the cat, obviously).

As soon as I was old enough (at age fifteen) I was off around England on my own, and then Europe, and later the world. I've always liked the idea of being some place that isn't home.

So, maybe I was born to be a traveller, but that doesn't explain why I became a writer. In fact, it's hard to find any clue in my family background that that's the path I would choose. Because – despite his travels, teaching credentials and Masters degree – Dad was definitely not a writer, and if we're looking for evidence we'll find it in the diary he kept of a trip he and my mother made in 1961 when they travelled overland in Ghana.

They set off from Takoradi, where they lived in the south, to Paga, the country's most northern town, on the Burkina Faso (then Upper Volta) border. This was an adventurous five-hundred-mile journey, in an Austin A40 loaded with enough tinned food for eight days, through an unfamiliar land that remained little developed outside the cities. It was true, off-the-beaten-track travel through a young, vibrant, post-colonial country, the first in Africa to gain independence. My parents were both trained teachers and must have been eager to see the country they called home. They travelled with an open mind and must have hoped to bring back memories of experiences that would last a lifetime.

After a full day on the road, Dad's diary entry from 27 December, 1961 reads, in full: "Takoradi. 5 gallons Shell."

Admit it, from this intricately woven word picture you can smell the dust on the ochre-red roads, feel the springs through the worn leather of the A40's seats, and sense the trickle of sweat down the back as the lush, green rain-forest forms a hundred-foot-high canopy above the corrugated highway.

The next day, 28 December, 1961, was Dad's thirty-first birthday, which I think is all the explanation needed for an entry that reads – otherwise bafflingly – "Kumasi. Odeon Garage – girls." Very broadminded of Mum, we have to agree, to allow that sort of thing during a break in the journey. However, whatever he was treated to at Kumasi's Odeon Garage, Dad didn't forget his other duties, since the diary also states – rather daringly given the previous day's consumption – "4 gallons Shell."

Kumasi is one of the most interesting places in Ghana, an old royal capital and cultural centre for the Ashanti people. Not for my parents, though, a tour of the city's fascinating sights, attractions, palaces, parks and museums. The diary just says, "It's too hot," and they both go to bed early, though not without Dad recording the name of the one significant historic and cultural attraction that they did visit, the Mampong Institute of Agriculture, where they must have had a right old time.

Two days later, he does record a market visit in Bolgatanga. I've been to markets in Ghana and they are extraordinary assaults on the senses, full of sights and smells that I have never encountered anywhere else in the world. I once saw a man in Kumasi market carrying a pig's head on both shoulders, which is the sort of thing you'd mention as an anecdote. I've never been to Bolgatanga but I'll bet there's all sorts of stuff going on there. However, Dad is made of sterner stuff and either doesn't give in to hyperbole or missed the whole pig's-head-carrying section of the market. "Blankets," says the diary. And "Smocks." Size, colour, bought, sold or stolen, we have no idea.

Later, there's the crossing of a flimsy toll bridge, where the Austin A40 has to be carefully manoeuvred over a fast-flowing river. Disaster could strike at any time, but luckily Dad has his eye on the crucial details. "Three fridges," he notes, and I think we can all breathe more easily knowing that.

On New Year's Eve, there's sensational news with the diary entry that reads simply "Navrongo – naked arrest." Which one of them it was, we have no way of knowing, but neither parent appears to have been detained for long because Dad gets positively garrulous with the rest of the entry for 31 December, going on to record "chickens for sale" at Paga.

Believe me, I've tried to imagine the set of circumstances that results in a naked, chicken-related incident that requires the presence of the Ghanaian police, but this is my parents we're talking about. There's only so far I want to glimpse into the heart of darkness.

Come the New Year and things go completely crazy. On 1 January, 1962, Dad's diary records "Damongo – 3 gallons Mobil." I know! He'd got to the town of Damongo and bought Mobil, not Shell! And down to three gallons! What was the man thinking?

So – a traveller then, undoubtedly, but not a writer. And in fact, a chip off the old literary block, since Dad had much in common with his own father, my paternal grandfather, Fred, whose diary I also happen to have.

Fred's early travelling life was just as adventurous, and even more dangerous, as he enlisted in the Royal Marines on 12 May, 1916, aged just seventeen years and ten months. He joined his first ship in July 1917, which is when his surviving diary begins, and sailed on to the Middle East and then Asia for a tour of duty that took in Baghdad, Mumbai, Sri Lanka, Singapore, Hong Kong and China.

The diary is another Brown family classic, and surely

inspired my father in his writings. Fred was in the vibrant trading port of Singapore, for example, on Saturday 24 September, 1917, where he and the ship's company "Took in 950 tons coal".

No mention of the grand scene at the harbour, or the colonial comforts of the Raffles Hotel; no appreciation of the climate or commerce; no comment about the dress, manner or characteristics of a local population that must have seemed strange, if not outlandish, to a teenager from Cambridge. Nope, Fred was all about the coal.

There was more taking in of coal in Hong Kong, and then a bit of to-ing and fro-ing as the diary breathlessly records how his ship "Left Hong Kong," "Arrived Singapore," "Left Singapore" and – can you guess? – "Arrived Hong Kong" again.

This continues for the next nine months – Fred dutifully recording the leaving and arriving, the anchoring and picking up of coal, and absolutely nothing else, as the Far East played out its buccaneering mercantile history in the dying days of the greatest conflict the world had ever seen.

If you wanted to know where all the coal was, Fred was your man. But otherwise, you wouldn't even know there was a war on from his diary.

That is, until Wednesday 12 June, 1918, when – according to his diary – my grandfather "Left at 11am to go pirate-hunting."

Wait, what?

We have to fill in the gaps, because Fred's diary is not what you'd call forthcoming, unless on the subject of coal. I don't suppose anyone had dwelt on the piracy issue when they first set off from England. "There'll be lots of coal to take on and off lads, and we'll probably do a bit of arriving and departing. Oh, and watch out for pirates. What? Nothing, no, carry on."

Unbeknownst to Fred at least, the China coast had been awash with pirates since the eighteenth century. Even in wartime, ports and ships were susceptible to raids and skirmishes, and the British forces in general and my grandad in particular were bound to encounter a pirate or two before long.

A few days later in June, after the pirate-hunting incident, Fred and his shipmates are recorded as "Searching junks" (ie, Chinese sailing ships). They must have found something because on Monday 17 June, 1918, the diary simply says:

"Shot fifteen pirates."

After that pithy bombshell the diary goes back to counting coal for a bit, though there's the drama of "Bad weather" on 7 August, before a final litany of "Arriving" at and "Leaving" various Chinese and Asian ports.

The final entry in the diary – Monday 23 February, 1920 – sees Fred safely home to a port in southeast England, after an extraordinary experience in anyone's eyes. He'd set off as a callow boy, a teenager, and returned having served as a participant and ringside spectator in the sprawling Asian theatre of the First World War. He'd unloaded coal in Singapore, survived a storm in the South China Sea, sailed in and out of Indian ports, defended the Empire, and apparently shot a bunch of pirates.

That, surely, would be a story worth telling and Fred, true to type, gives it his all and writes from the heart:

"Arrived Chatham."

I don't tell you any of these things to make fun of my dad, Ken, and Fred, the grandfather I never knew, though these diaries make me howl with laughter when I consider the spaces between the (very few) words that contain the most extraordinary of adventures and experiences.

Bless them both, really, I wouldn't have them any other way.

Their examples – the family tradition, you could say – might well have made me the traveller I am. Go on, let's say they definitely did. But where did the 'writer' in travel writer come from?

The answer to that lies in one more diary, written by my mother, Jean, in 1961, shortly after her arrival in Ghana. She was twenty-three years old, had just been on her first ever aeroplane, was terrified of thunderstorms and spiders, and was wearing a long-sleeved cardigan in the tropical heat because she had been warned about the dangers of mosquitoes.

This is what she wrote, a few days later:

> *A large frog hopped around my feet as I stepped outside the airport. Huge scarlet flowers and spiky banana-like leaves flared above the green of the grass, while bright birds scrambled and sang, turning shade*

into light for a darting moment. Farther away the ground sloped and I could see palm trees growing thickly and heavily against the pale pewter sky. Standing near the car were several children gazing at the airfield. They wore brilliant robes wrapped carelessly and gracefully around them, their feet were bare, and their dark, deep eyes glimmered in smooth, brown faces. They stared curiously at us in our thick winter clothes, then they smiled and touched their foreheads. We smiled back and then were whirled away from the airport, and our stay in Africa had begun.

Later, when she'd visited her first market, in the city of Takoradi where I would be born a year later, she had more diary observations to make, that went far beyond my Dad's blankets-and-smocks description.

 Sitting on the step of a dark doorway is an old man patiently embroidering a skullcap with tiny, delicate stitches. Squatting by a nearby wall, a man has a typewriter balanced on a board on his knees. He will type any letter for two shillings — one such letter, written for a man who was applying to be taken on as a labourer, began, "I have hopefully to beg with respect, Sir..." and ended with the applicant's mark of a cross. The noise is tremendous, a high-pitched chatter of voices, with loud laughter echoing everywhere. All the women and many of the men wear the traditional 'kente' dress, long, brightly patterned robes wrapped around the waist and flung over the shoulder.

Or the men wear a white, sack-like garment, sleeveless and embroidered upwards in tucks from the waist. The tiny children wear nothing at all.

Mum wrote those things, off the cuff, effortlessly and gracefully, about the first exotic place she ever visited, for no one's pleasure other than her own. She recorded facts and figures when she learned them – the daily wages of labourers, hut-building methods, farming practices – and had an eye for a scene that any travel writer would relish.

The slaughterhouse is elaborately domed and minareted, and could at first glance be confused with the mosque, were it not for the vultures. These cluster thickly, fringing the building with their black bodies and bald, grey-pink heads. It is a fascinating sight as they wheel slowly in the air and circle down to rest before diving into the building – apart from the domes, it is roofless. Nearby are the rough pens for the animals destined for slaughter – thin sheep and goats, and humpbacked cattle with enormous horns like Highland cows.

She later had a couple of articles published in her old local paper, the *Derby Evening Telegraph*, and another piece in the *Guardian* (receiving the princely sum of twelve guineas). But otherwise all Mum's writing was in private travel journals and diaries that she put together for friends and family after every trip, spanning almost fifty years.

That's travelling *and* writing. Mum would have told us more about the pirates and so would I. So, if you want to know if this travel writer was born or made, I'd say the answer lies with Fred, Ken and Jean, two gallons of Shell and a ton of coal.

PART TWO
BONUS CHAPTERS

TRAVEL + WRITER: AN INSIDER'S GUIDE

When people ask me what it's like to be a travel writer, I never really know what to say. I've done it for so long that it's as if they are asking what it's like to be me. The answer to which is – long periods in front of a computer, random thoughts about football and snacks, periodic bursts of anxiety, some mucking about on Twitter, and travelling to places now and again.

I think what people really mean is – is travelling for a living as exciting as it sounds? The answer to which is – sometimes yes and sometimes no.

For most of my writing life I was a guidebook writer, sent around the world for Rough Guides, which was exciting because I'd never been to places such as Norway, Hong Kong or Washington DC before, and here was someone asking me to go there and write a book about it. Not only that, I was going to get paid to travel, which at first seemed to me like someone had made an error somewhere. I certainly wasn't about to tell them that, so I kept quiet and turned into a travel writer.

On the other hand, travelling regularly around the world involves lots of packing, waiting around, missing connections, finding places to stay and eat, and generally doing the sorts of things you do at home, only doing them in a foreign country where you don't always know what's going on.

It's not all bar-crawling in Barcelona, bungee-jumping in New Zealand, and trekking in Nepal, is what I'm saying. Those are the exciting bits. Everything else can be a bit of a hassle, especially – as a guidebook writer – if you also have to write it all down so that your readers have the best information available. I might have got on the wrong bus to the wrong town (more often than you'd think), but it was my job to make sure that you didn't. And no one ever mistook a travel writer standing at a bus stop in the rain copying down a timetable for someone living their best life.

That said, after thirty-five years as a travel writer, I figure that I finally have a handle on the day-to-day bits of the job. Getting around, putting together hotel reviews, finding decent restaurants to recommend, researching destinations, writing inspiring accounts of sights and attractions – that's really what being a travel writer is like for me, most of the time.

So in these bonus chapters, I thought I'd let you in behind the scenes and share some of the insider secrets of the travel-writing trade. I hope you find them useful or at least entertaining because – for better or worse – this is what I've chosen to do with my life. Travel, and then write about it for readers like you.

It's a tough job but someone has to do it and that someone turned out to be me. I still can't quite believe that they gave the job to the right person, but let's keep that between ourselves.

SIX THINGS YOU SHOULD
NEVER LEAVE HOME
WITHOUT

I HAVE a little rubber plug for a bathroom sink that I take with me on every trip. It used to come in handy, back in the days when I regularly stayed in the sort of hotels that either didn't expect their guests to wash properly or didn't want their guests to do laundry in the room.

To be honest, the lack of a sink-plug was often the least of my worries in a place like that. I once stayed in a cheap guest house in Portugal with the toilet sited right in the middle of the room, conveniently next to the bed. In Australia, I actually spent one night *in* a toilet, when the rest of the hostel had flooded. And in Macau, the room above the casino came with the added but dubious benefit of prostitutes trying the door every ten minutes to see if I minded giving them some space so that they could carry out their work.

Still, packing the plug meant that I could shave and wash properly in many a budget hotel around the world, and I've continued to take it with me, even though now I simply call the hotel barber from my super king-sized four-poster and have new clothes sent up daily.

When people ask me for packing tips, I always mention the plug, at which point their faces fall as they realise that, just because I'm a travel writer doesn't mean that I know what I'm talking about. I think they're expecting that I have a system involving zip-lock vacuum packs and rolling T-shirts into tubes, but I don't. I just stuff it all in a twenty-year-old backpack and sit on it a bit to squash it down.

However, I don't like to disappoint, so I had another think and came up with six things that travellers should never leave home without. Best of all, they don't cost anything. Not that it should set you back more than a few pennies, if you really liked the plug idea.

Patience. You'll need a lot of it. Don't stint.

At some point, your train will be late. Or your flight will be delayed. Or the shop will be closed for no apparent reason. Or a national holiday will get in the way of your plans.

Take a deep breath. This unfortunate delay or occurrence is part of what you came for – a chance to experience the irregular rhythms of a foreign country and a different way of life.

Some of my most memorable experiences have been *mañana* moments – hanging around, waiting for something to happen or for somewhere to open. An unplanned night in Kuala Lumpur because the incoming flight was late; four days on an Italian island while storms grounded the ferry fleet; forty-eight hours on a train from Barcelona to England because an erupting Icelandic volcano stopped every flight in Europe. I mean, you couldn't make the last one up – a volcano eruption, it's the best 'dog ate my homework' travel excuse of all time.

Any event like this starts out as tiresome and frustrating – you just want to get home, catch the train, go shopping, do the thing you'd planned to do. You could get cross and let it ruin your day, but it's not going to change the situation. Instead, accept and transcend, people, accept and transcend.

It wouldn't be Spain if they didn't close everything down for four hours in the middle of the day – they're not doing it just to annoy you. It wouldn't be China if they didn't ignore you and serve everyone else first – they just don't want to lose face by having to deal with a foreigner that they can't understand.

Be patient. Don't see delays and obstructions as spoiling your trip, see them as part of your trip. Thrown together on replacement buses or waiting in line for somewhere to open or someone to serve you, you'll have chance encounters, meet interesting people, and get some fascinating glimpses of day-to-day life. They'll make for much stronger memories.

And the bonus, for a travel writer, of these unplanned stops and disastrous journeys? Each is a potential story, mine to tell in my own way. I just try and be patient, and let the experiences and stories come to me.

An open mind will get you further in your travels than an open wallet. I just made that aphorism up, but I think it's true.

It's about opening yourself up to opportunities, so that you'll see more of the world and have wider, better travel experiences. It isn't always about the trips you can buy or the adventures you can pay for.

Sometimes, you just need to say, "Oh all right then, I'll have a go," whether it's eating something unfamiliar or joining in with the dancing at a local festival.

Don't say, "I don't like … " when what you mean is, "I've never tried …"

Be alert to every possibility. Say "Yes" and "Why not?" – not "No" and "You must be kidding."

Try new things. Do different stuff. Go against your own grain. In fact, it's often easier to do these things when you're away, where no one knows you. You have a one-time chance to reinvent yourself as a chilli-chomp-ing, morris-dancing, snake-handling, yoga enthusiast, and if you really don't like it then no one at home will ever be any the wiser. But at least you gave it a go.

Travelling with an open mind is also about leaving your preconceptions at home. It's easy to stereotype certain countries or nationalities – we all do it, even when we think we're scrupulous about not doing it. But the one thing at least that travel should do is open our minds to the common humanity of others. Travelling with an open mind means looking beyond walls, borders and languages, and seeing people and places with a genuine interest and curiosity.

If you do that as a visitor, you'll get more out of every place that you go. Meanwhile, the best travel writing takes you to the true heart of a destination, and the best travel writers do that by writing with an open heart and mind.

A few words in the local language go a long way to opening doors, smoothing paths and finding your way.

"Please" and "Thank you" in any language shouldn't be beyond anyone – and really, if you're not prepared to learn to say "Thank you," then maybe you'd be better off staying at home. If you can manage "Can you pass me the soap dish?" and "Where is the bus shelter?" (as I can, inexplicably, in Dutch and German respectively) then people smile and you'll go far.

There are limits, of course. On a visit to Moscow, my friend bought an old phrasebook that dated back to the 1980 Olympic Games and for a week all he could say was, "Which way is the pole-vaulting event, please?" and other similarly unhelpful sentences. It took him days to find his way to Red Square.

If you don't have a phrasebook, you'll usually be able to get by with pointing and Google Translate, but that isn't really the issue. It's about making an effort to be understood – even at a very minimal level – in a place where you're a stranger. No one will expect you to be able to hold an in-depth conversation – though if you can, go you! – but taking the trouble to be polite is a basic human requirement for a traveller.

Talking of which …

Load yourself up with good manners.

They do things differently in foreign countries. They just do. And while not all of those things might seem sensible or reasonable to you, that's just how they do them, so you should follow suit and not complain endlessly.

You're a guest and a visitor and, while you'll usually be given plenty of leeway if you genuinely didn't know you were supposed to bow, or eat with a particular hand, or take your shoes off, there's no call to ignore customs and upset people just because it doesn't seem right to you.

Not making eye contact on the Tube in London, for example – hard to bear for a cheery Texan or Italian, but seriously, keep your head down and for God's sake don't actually try and talk to a Londoner, you'll only worry them.

I get that not everything is right in some countries, at least as far as you and your personal views are concerned. If you have strong feelings about capital punishment, women's rights, gun control, or religious and political freedom, then you may also have strong feelings about visiting certain countries. It's your choice, of course, and I'm not making suggestions one way or the other. I think we all come to some accommodation with ourselves about the places we choose to visit; we all make value judgements; we all occasionally close our eyes to something if it gets in the way of a good trip.

But if you genuinely can't countenance a particular world view or a set of political circumstances, then perhaps you shouldn't go in the first place, it's that simple.

For all other customs and attitudes, you should follow the lead of the locals, whether it's turning right on a red light in the USA ("What, now? Are you mad?"), barging to the front of any queue in Ireland ("Ah sure, it's grand") or eating dinner at midnight in Spain ("You mean at bedtime?"). These all seem like outlandish ideas to me, but I do them anyway without complaint, it's just good manners.

Dust down your sense of curiosity; it may not have been used for a while.

What's down that street? Where is that procession going? What can I see from the top of the hill? Is that church open? Does kangaroo really taste like chicken? Is the North Sea really that cold? (Sort of, and yes, to the last two, in case you were wondering.)

It pays to be endlessly curious about the world and the opportunities it presents. The most interesting finds are often the unexpected ones, or those for which you have to work harder. That backstreet restaurant that's not in the guidebook; that town you only stayed in because you liked the sound of its name; the museum that was open when all the famous ones were closed – serendipity, that's often what makes for great travel experiences, combined with your willingness to turn another corner or try another direction.

These accidental discoveries are the things that will stay with you, long after your trip is over. You'll probably tell other people about them too, though go easy because other people's travel stories are notoriously uninteresting.

For travel writers, though, curiosity is part of the job description and telling people about your holidays is not only allowed but positively encouraged. My very task is to make you want to go somewhere. My job is to turn my curiosity into a few hundred well-chosen words that, in turn, will inspire someone I've never met – hi there! – to travel to new places and try new experiences.

I hope it's going well so far.

Your bag's getting full, I know, but before you finally set off on your travels, try squeezing in a spirit of generosity before departure.

If you can afford to fly away somewhere for a few days, or have the money to travel around Asia for six months, you can afford whatever it is you're going to quibble about next. This isn't about haggling *per se* – haggle away, fill your boots, you're unlikely to come out on top against a professional market-trader or storekeeper.

This is about not being an idiot – about those long and vociferous arguments between travellers and locals, or even traveller-on-traveller, about how it's a con and they are definitely not paying that outrageous extra ten cents.

Don't ever find yourself being that person. Tips for waiters and room-cleaners, cash for buskers, alms for beggars, rounding up fares for drivers – let's not be mean when it comes to people's livelihoods. Buy a fellow traveller a drink, spread some money around at the neighbourhood market, get your host a gift, drop some change in the donations box, give the local kids a treat – you can afford it, you'll help someone out, and maybe you'll make a new travel memory or two.

And now you're fully packed, you're good to go. You've got your patience, open mind, good manners, sense of curiosity, spirit of generosity, and even a few words in the local language.

Ready to travel?

FINDING A ROOM AT THE END OF THE WORLD

WRITING MY FIRST GUIDEBOOK, the *Rough Guide to Scandinavia*, I turned up in the Swedish city of Malmö, where the tourist board had arranged a night's stay in a hotel for me. This was still a novelty – that someone would put me up for free in a hotel and all I had to do was write about how nice it was. I was a backpacker traveller. 'Nice' was a hostel dorm room where no one snored or farted all night long. Hotels, especially Swedish hotels, were not in my budget. Consequently, I didn't have the greatest of expectations, but it was free and that was good enough for me.

I hoisted my backpack on one shoulder and followed the clerk down a mahogany-lined corridor, further and further into the hotel. We passed signs pointing the way to the room numbers, went up a couple of floors in an unmarked elevator, and then walked along a deeply carpeted corridor with just one door at the end of it. As we got closer, it became apparent that the sign on the door said 'Royal Suite' and, instead of veering right past and opening up a hidden box-room, the clerk took an enormous metal key out of his jacket, opened the door and beckoned me in.

"This is where our King and Queen stay," he announced. "Please, make yourself at home."

He managed to maintain a poker face as I dumped my worn backpack onto some embroidered, eighteenth-century bedside chest, made his excuses and left – doubt-less, straight on the phone to the Swedish Tourist Board to ask what they thought they were playing at.

The rest of the trip went downhill from there. Maybe the tourist board mis-read 'Rough' as 'Royal,' who knows, but after a night in an antique-filled, harbour-view suite, it was back to the snorers and farters in the hostel dorms. (Though not before dinner in the hotel's lavish restaurant where the sommelier – clearly made of sterner stuff than the clerk – asked what I wanted to drink and when I said, "A bottle of red wine," replied with heavy emphasis, "A *small glass* of red wine, very good Sir.")

As an introduction to the travel-writing life, my royal retreat was obviously amazing good luck but proved to be a totally useless experience as far as writing budget guide-books went. I can't imagine it was any use at all either to the fancy hotel or the Swedish Tourist Board, when my two-line review finally saw the light of day. I can't remember exactly, but given the Rough Guides tell-it-like it-is vibe it was almost certainly along the lines of "Nice hotel with a mean sommelier. Request the royal suite. No idea what it costs, ask the tourist board."

Instead, my bread and butter was inspecting and sleeping in little, family-run pensions, guest houses and basic hotels so that I could describe them to readers. It was a big part of the job and quite the responsibility, given that people would plan their trips and book their accommodation on the basis of my simple reviews in a guidebook.

But you're very possibly reading this, not under-standing a word of what I'm trying to convey. Guidebook hotel recommendations? OK boomer, what is this, of which you speak?

Booking a hotel room in a foreign land used to be a hazardous business. There wasn't much support out there. You had to take things on trust. Who knew what you were really going to get, when all you had to go on was a photo in a brochure? A brochure given to you by a travel agent who had never been to the hotel but was getting a commission for booking you in there. A travel agent, yes. You know, with a shop on the high street? Yes, a shop, you must … never mind.

Who knew if 'bathroom' meant a bath, a shower or a bucket in the middle of the floor, or if the touted 'view' was actually of the car park and not the Colosseum? Who knew if that really was the price you'd end up paying when you got there? The guidebook was all you had. You couldn't Google the place, or message them, or send them an email. You might ring them, I suppose, but who was going to ring Sweden? You could fax them, possibly. You know, a fax? Oh, never mind.

Over the years, I got really good at working out which

were the nicer places to stay in lots of European cities and then wrote about them in guidebooks. I described them as well as I could, picking out the details that differentiated one cheap place from another. Sometimes I spent whole days just looking in hotel rooms, deciding if I'd want to stay there – in which case, I could probably recommend them as an option to someone else. I acquired an eye for natural light, potential street noise, whether the shower looked as if it was any good, and a dozen other things.

I hope some people found all that useful. At least, no one ever complained to me about Malmö's royal suite. And because I think it's a handy skill to have, I'm going to share some tips. These might save your life one day – well, find you a decent, cheap room for the night anyway, which often amounts to the same thing when you're travelling.

Bear with me here. Let's just pretend that the internet is down and you don't have your phone. (Don't panic. It's just pretend. You don't need to start hyperventilating and stocking up on tinned food.)

And let's also pretend that you've been set down in a foreign European city, with little or none of the local language, and a tight budget. You can't just go and get some more money from the ATM because ATMs don't exist. You've just got the cash in your wallet or purse.

Head between your knees, that's it. Breathe deeply. You're fine, really. Ready?

Right, for starters, don't listen to the man at the train station/bus station/ferry port. I say this reluctantly, because obviously not everyone is out to fleece you. I don't want you to distrust the first person you meet in a place, as a matter of course. In some countries and destinations, it's perfectly fine to jump on the back of someone's scooter and go and see their "cousin's guesthouse, very close, very cheap – everywhere else already full."

I'm just saying that, on the whole, this option removes the control from you and grants it to the man on the scooter, who is now driving you to a satellite suburb several time zones away, where his cousin's guesthouse (well, not strictly his cousin, more like his boss, but let's not quibble) – while perfectly fine – is A) a bit pricey and B) no, you can't have a lift back if you don't like it. Also, and probably no spoiler, everywhere else wasn't already full.

Use your common sense, that's all you need to do. Greek island harbour, middle of summer, lots of tourists competing for rooms and lots of cheery touts, probably an all-right deal. City-centre train station, pushy guy with space-encroachment issues, probably not.

You don't need him anyway, you need the old town, because in Europe the cheapest places to stay are always in the old town. Not sure where that is? Head for the cathedral or main square and start scouting around the back streets – you'll soon turn up the sort of places that don't appear on any price-comparison site. We're talking small, individually owned places – an historic building or a few rooms in an apartment, a sign and a buzzer. Let's not worry about the buzzer for now. I know, you don't speak the language, but it will be fine.

So, you've found a likely looking place. Now ask to see a room – it's not considered rude and, at this end of the market, is expected. I wouldn't have a look at Malmö's royal suite and then ask to see another room ("Have you got anything nicer?"), but it will be acceptable to do that here, in our budget hotel.

Some rooms, it turns out, are much better than others for the same price, so it pays to shop around. The owners – the little blighters and minxes – might try and fill the worst ones first, especially if you're on your own. However, most won't mind showing you a room or two, and you can have a look in the bathroom and check the view while you're at it. Does it look clean? Can you – as per *Fawlty Towers* – see herds of wildebeest sweeping majestically across the plain, or is the view of a brick wall? If the owner just gives you the key and doesn't come with you, I'd also have a surreptitious bounce on the bed. Who wants to sleep on springs? Run the taps as well? Why not.

Here's the thing. If you don't like the room, the view, the bed or the water pressure, you don't have to stay there. You haven't booked in advance, paid a deposit or committed to a no-refund price. Smile nicely, say thank you and move on.

Feel awkward? Want an excuse? Say, "I'll have to check with my friend." You don't even have to have a friend. It's a code, they all know. Travelling around Italy, I learned the Italian word for wife, *moglie*, which I refer-enced with a shrug on such occasions. The owner would tap their nose – understood, you don't have executive authority in these matters, who does?

And to emphasize the point that you'll only know if you have a look in advance, I booked a budget room online relatively recently that gave up its hidden secret on arrival. "This room does not have a window," it said, in very, very small print at the bottom of the terms-and-conditions page, which was true and legal but very, very annoying, having paid in advance and got there late at night. Funnily enough, there had also been no mention of the smell – think slaughterhouse drainage system – which, in a small, windowless room, made for a sleepless night of fever-murder dreams.

Back to the buzzer-language business. Sure, with the phone app you don't need to know anything. But there's been a planet-zapping, electro-magnetic pulse, remember, and your phone and Google Translate are very much 'service unavailable.' Don't worry, you still don't need to know anything. Their business is rooms. You're standing there, pushing a buzzer at a rooms' place. They have rooms. You want one. They'll let you in and you'll figure it out, especially if you've taken the trouble to learn a word or two in the local language. Bathroom, breakfast, double bed, single bed, shower, balcony, view, price – you don't need much more than this to find a room anywhere in the world.

Wait, there is one more phrase you could master. "Have you got anything cheaper?" is not necessarily an invitation to show you the broom cupboard. Rooms without an en-suite bathroom are always cheaper, as are rooms up in the attic. Or perhaps there are internal rooms that overlook an airshaft or inner courtyard and not the sweeping herds of wildebeest.

"Is breakfast included?" could be another question, while you're at it. Breakfast in a budget hotel in much of Europe is pointless, a croissant or a cellophane-wrapped packet of dry toast and a cup of weak coffee, served in the only corner of the building that they couldn't make into another room. I'd go to the neighbourhood bar instead, it'll be much more fun, and if you don't have the hotel breakfast they might knock a bit of money off the price of the room.

Ultimately, if it saves you some cash, you might be happy with any of these options, or you might not be, but there's no harm in checking.

Now you've found your room and are happy with it, there's really not much else to tell you. Dump your bags, go and get some lunch, that would be my advice.

You might not want to commit to a longer stay until you've spent at least a night there, just in case the church bells opposite chime all night on the hour or the hotel lies on the crack-of-dawn bin-cleaning route. But on the whole, you've done your due diligence and can relax – apart from the bit where they ask you to leave your passport with them and you fear it will be sold to an underworld grifter the minute you turn your back. Don't worry, they're just filling in whatever forms they have to by law, and it's guaranteed – well, ninety percent certain, all right, eighty – that you'll get your passport back when you return from lunch. Welcome to your character-filled, budget hotel room in old-town Europe.

How much use these insights are for anyone under the age of forty is debatable. It probably doesn't even compute that you might choose to tramp around Barcelona, say, and look in a few hotel rooms on the morning of your arrival. You've seen the photos on the phone app, booking website or Instagram, read the reviews, chatted to the hotel, and already made your decision, booked and paid. Even your parents probably travel like that. I travel like that these days, and I'm so old that although my parents had a computer, it was of the vintage that meant it got covered with a shawl like a revered icon when not in use – ie, all the time. They had a mobile phone, too, which was not at all mobile because they kept it permanently stationed in a drawer for unspecified 'emergencies.'

Consequently, any advice I have is probably on a par with one of those medieval, medical manuscripts recommending leech-application for a headache.

But I do have one more bit of hotel-related wisdom that might help, even if your generation doesn't have a letter yet. It's the number one golden rule for avoiding unexpected charges that negate the whole point of staying in a cheap hotel in the first place. I learned the hard way, on a trip to Iceland with some fellow travel writers, where a boisterous night out continued after-hours in my hotel room.

"Oh look, a fridge," said Travel Writer A, whereupon

Travel Writers B, C and D emptied it of its contents and the wild rumpus began.

You can only have a real idea of how expensive a country is when you are presented with a bill in the morning for little bottles of alcohol, number – or indeed contents – uncertain.

Never, ever, ever use the mini-bar.

That's it. In the end, that's the best advice I have for you, as you unpack in your newly acquired hotel room. Splash out on a view, order the champagne breakfast, upgrade to a suite, stay for a month, but under no circumstances open so much as a packet of peanuts without checking the small print.

TOURIST OR TRAVELLER?

I USE THE WORD 'TRAVELLER' a lot – hard to avoid in a book about travel – and I use it in its general, literal sense, 'someone who travels.' But you'll doubtless have seen many articles and blogs which articulate the supposed differences between a 'tourist' and a 'traveller.' It's a common trope in the travel community, and we all know what they mean – just take a look at the Twitter feeds of those travellers, nomads, backpackers, wander-lusters, roamers, gypsies and adventurers.

You go on holiday. They are experiencing real life. You're a tourist. They're a traveller. The implication being that the first is a terrible thing to be – the resorts, the noise, the people! – and the second a much more noble enterprise. As if a city break in Paris or week's holiday on the Algarve is somehow less valuable an experience than travelling overland to Istanbul, trekking in Morocco, or blogging from a Vietnamese beach. 'Travellers' have 'authentic' experiences, they get 'off the beaten track', and they are absolutely, definitely not on holiday – heavens, no – but seeing the 'real' country instead.

It's not a new attitude. Writer G.K. Chesterton pontificated:

"The traveller sees what he sees. The tourist sees what he has come to see."

Or here's Paul Theroux – the blessed Paul, proper traveller, proper writer – giving it the full sniff:

"Tourists don't know where they've been, travellers don't know where they're going."

They are both saying the same rather patronising thing, which is that it's somehow better to be a traveller than a tourist.

If you are an actual explorer – a hammock-in-the-jungle kinda guy, a tent-in-the-desert gal – with a wander-lust that knows no boundaries and an urge to roam that's dredged from your very soul, then 'traveller' is probably fair enough. Some of the greatest travel books have been written by such people, providing fascinating philosoph-ical insights into the way that Planet Earth's peoples live. Wilfrid Thesiger, Geoffrey Moorhouse, Bruce Chatwin, Dervla Murphy, Jan Morris – these are all writers who could call themselves travellers without anyone rolling their eyes.

Ultimately, I don't mind what people call themselves if it makes them happy. Traveller. Wanderer. Whatever. Well, there's one I do mind – if you're going to call your-self a 'digital nomad,' I want to see you with a camel as well as a laptop.

But let's be honest. Everyone else is basically a tourist – a tripper, holidaymaker, sightseer, visitor, excursionist, if you want to look it up in the dictionary. And what's more, this used to be a good thing.

It was once quite the height of sophistication to be a tourist. A Grand Tour of Europe was *de rigueur* for a wealthy young person in the eighteenth and nineteenth century. To be a 'tourist' was to be a person of taste and means. You certainly weren't on holiday – that would have been a stay on your country estate or a retreat to the spa pavilion. 'Travellers' were traders, working people, on-the-road stiffs, who had to stick to the nine to five (or, more likely, the dawn to dusk) to earn a living. You, on the other hand, were touring Europe to have an experience and, as a tourist, you were one of the fortunate, one of the favoured.

You still are, of course. If you can afford a holiday then, whatever you call yourself, you're lucky to travel, to be able to afford to visit beautiful, interesting and distant places.

Thinking of yourself as a tourist keeps you grounded. It reminds you that not everyone has this opportunity, not least half the people in half the countries you visit, where they really don't care if you're a nomad or an adventurer, as long as you spend money in their guest house or restaurant. Because tourism – not travellerism – is paying their bills.

As a travel writer, it also pays to have some self-awareness, because readers can see straight through any inauthenticity. I'm in no doubt. Wherever I go and for however long, I'm not a 'traveller' inducted into some arcane priesthood. I'm not a 'nomad' with secret knowledge and special skills.

I'm a tourist, visiting somewhere for pleasure – my own and the readers. I'm a guest in another country, for a short or a longer period, and then I'm going home again, where I'll tell people all about my holiday, for a holiday is what it really was.

Not being precious about this truth allows me to tell other truths: What is this place really like for a visitor? Did I enjoy it? Would I recommend it to someone else? Is there a story to tell?

And then the best I'm going to be able to do is give you a snapshot of my time in whichever destination it was. And, because I'm a writer, I'll be able to make it sound interesting, exciting or adventurous, depending on my mood and style.

So, telling the truth about being a tourist makes me a better traveller – in its very general sense. And telling truths about travel is the job of a good travel writer.

Tourist (noun) – a person who is travelling or visiting a place for pleasure.

Tourist. That will do me.

AWESOME HIDDEN GEMS IN
A LAND OF CONTRASTS

THERE IS A LAND, far, far away – let's call it Clichénia –
where travel writers spend more time than they should.
Its siren call – echoing across panoramic vistas and
sweeping through timeless villages – lures the travelling
hacks to a charmed Mecca where mere everyday words
and phrases are not enough to describe the awesome
wonders that confront them.

In Clichénia, descriptive words must be wrought from
a bejewelled mine. They must be words that dazzle,
words that speak of the bustling and buzzing best-kept
secrets to which the travel writer, and the travel writer
alone – oh, lucky travel writer – bears witness.

All these words and phrases can be found in a dictionary issued to travel writers on their first day on the job.
A copy has – mysteriously – fallen into my hands, and I
thought I'd share some of its secrets with you here. For a
bit of fun, feel free to play 'Travel Writer Bingo' the next
time you read a travel book or blog.

'A land of contrasts,' the oldest of old favourites, is used to describe anywhere with some mountains and a coast-line, for example, or lots of big cities and – hang on, that's unusual – lots of small villages as well. Or rich people and – well, darn me – poor people too.

If you can go skiing in the morning and head to the beach in the afternoon, then that, my friends, is a land of contrasts. If the capital city (let's say London) has hipster cafés and skyscrapers and the countryside (how about Yorkshire?) has green fields and sheep, then I think we all know what kind of land England is.

Let's be honest though, everywhere could be described as a land of contrasts, from Belgium to New Zealand. Well, maybe not stereotypically flat and dull Belgium. I got into trouble once for comparing (unfavourably) a genuine if perplexing museum, the Museum of Illustrious Catalans, with a supposed Museum of Famous Belgians. A right royal hoo-ha ensued, as Belgian readers sent me comprehensive lists of well-known Belgians such as the Flemish artists Van Eyck and Rubens and I countered with the fact that they weren't Belgian, because the country didn't exist until 1830, and the entire hot mess continued until I got down off my high horse and apolo-gised for my lazy, simplistic jibe. And just to show what I know, the highest point in Belgium is almost a whopping 2,300 feet, which is only a thousand feet below England's, and we already know that England is a land of contrasts.

Anyway, I digress. Frankly, my back garden is a land of contrasts. It has both flowers and trees. But no one would be thrilled to be lured to my back garden, instead of Patagonia for example, so let's ignore that one straight away.

'Something for everyone' crops up quite a lot, or – as a wise person once said to me – 'Nothing for anyone.' We're all different, we don't all like the same things, and we don't all have the same tastes. So using this phrase to recommend an attraction that my five-year-old child or my granny will love doesn't help me in the slightest, because Peppa Pig and garden centres are not big in my world.

The world's most famous department store, Harrods, conceivably, has something for everyone – last time I checked you could buy a yacht as well as a bar of soap. Heaven, too, probably caters for all tastes and require-ments. The Open-Air Farming and Vintage Doll Museum doesn't.

'Step back in time' – ah yes, apart from the cars, the satellite dishes, the people with cell phones, the window frames with actual glass in them, the concrete and the traffic lights. The writer means the place is old and attractive. Probably medieval, if in Europe. Probably nineteenth century, if in America.

If there are cows in the road, we have not stepped back in time, we're just in modern-day India. Or Cornwall. And in any case, stepping back in time would be rubbish. We're going to die of dysentery, or be burned at the stake because we laughed when they said the world was flat.

Unless we literally emerged from a time portal, in which case the phrase is allowed, please don't tell us we've stepped back in time. Travel writers would be better describing the scene instead, so we know what to expect.

"The cobbled streets and ancient stone buildings are charming, especially at night when they are lit by the cleansing fires and echo with the screams of a thousand heretics," that sort of thing.

We're out for dinner, and I see we are enjoying a meal in the 'family-run restaurant.'

Here's the travel writer's thought process. There's an old guy in charge, doing the front-of-house stuff. And a woman of about the same age, working the stoves out back. And the waiter is the age their son would be, if they had a son. That's really all they've got to go on.

Basically, if we're being told it's family-run, we want to see birth and marriage certificates. And then we want to know why a familial relationship makes them cook and serve the food better than in the restaurant run by the wage slaves next door. The Borgias were family. Would we want to have eaten in their restaurant?

While we're here, is this restaurant apparently full of 'locals'? See above – demand to see ID from everyone showing place of birth or residence before you accept this description.

Or are you following the travel writer's advice by eating in a 'local restaurant,' family-run or otherwise – as in, "Don't miss a meal in this great local restaurant." That's lucky for you. All the Michelin-starred restaurants in this street teleport themselves daily to random destinations, but this one stays put in its local location – it's terrible, but at least you can always find it.

Is there a more alluring description than 'hidden gem'? No one else knows this place exists, except the travel writer and now you.

This one is actually very simple.

Usage allowable if, Indiana Jones-like, you abseiled down a thousand-foot cliff, crossed a fraying rope bridge, and swam across waters teeming with barracuda to discover a hitherto-unknown medieval town backed by a white sandy beach.

Not allowable if you travelled somewhere quite nice on the bus that was in the guidebook. Or if your auntie told you about it after she got back from her cruise. Also, not applicable to a backstreet restaurant where you happen to be the only customer. It's not a hidden gem, it's just not very good.

Closely related to hidden gem is 'off the beaten track.'

This is a destination so fiendishly difficult to reach that it's in every guidebook and travel article ever written.

You'll know it when you get there, because it will be packed with people getting off tour buses and out of rental cars, clutching guidebooks and travel articles. It won't be down an actual track either, because that invalidates your car rental insurance for a start. And to be honest, I'd be surprised if the *beaten* track you went down, before you went *off* the beaten track, was actually beaten by native peoples with wooden paddles and brushes – it was probably tarmac, put down by the Council.

We will be hungry and thirsty when we reach our off-the-beaten-track, hidden-gem destination, but fortunately there are establishments that will serve us food and drink. These aren't restaurants, cafés or bars – oh no, they are 'eateries' and 'hostelries.'

No one knows why. They might have a regular menu, but equally they could be offering 'fayre' which, unless you've time-travelled to the Middle Ages (or 'stepped back in time'), just means a toasted sandwich and not a whole, spit-roasted pig with an apple in its mouth.

(It is entirely different in Italy, by the way. When it's time to eat long, thin strands of pasta, you can visit a 'spaghetteria' or when you fancy a beer you go to a 'birreria.' I promise, I haven't made them up, those are real Italian words. The writer is allowed to use those.)

Eateries and hostelries, by the way, only serve 'traditional' or 'authentic' food and drink. Generally, that isn't foraged, hedgerow salads, the meat from grain-fed, rare-breed animals, and first-press organic cider. It's burgers, lasagne, a Thai green curry and a pint of Irish Guinness (brewed in Malaysia).

Conversely, even if the eatery does serve genuinely authentic, traditional food, you won't like it – witness the hoo-ha about *paella* in its spiritual home of Valencia. Everyone likes a chicken and seafood *paella*, only the Valencians insist that isn't a proper dish at all, because an *echt* paella is made with snails, rabbit and green beans. Exactly, who wants that?

We've checked into the Hotel Clichénia, as recommended in the guidebook, where there's confusing news about the room.

Our accommodation for the night is 'nestled' on the edge of a 'verdant' jungle but doesn't have anything as commonplace as a view. Instead, it has – well, actually, 'boasts' – a 'majestic,' nay, 'breath-taking' 'panorama' or 'vista.'

We're exhausted just reading that, trying to unpick

the experience that we're being promised. And 'boasts,' what's going on there? People boast, hotels don't, not unless we're in the twenty-third century and Holiday Inn has achieved sentience.

How's the room, by the way? Bit on the small side? 'Cosy,' by any chance? If you ever read that the rooms are cosy, you can bank on being able to touch all four walls by stretching your limbs out from the bed. If it's also described as 'spartan,' it won't be entirely devoid of luxury or comfort – it probably just doesn't have a picture on the wall or a rug on the floor. See also 'minimalist.'

When we tire of the vista, it's time to head down to the waterside restaurant and beach bar, which apparently have a 'ramshackle' air. Rather than being ruinous and decrepit, I think what the travel writer means to say here is that there are some raffia-work chairs and old farm implements on display.

Vista, panorama, spartan, nestled, ramshackle, verdant – mark these words well. They are only ever used by travel writers, not normal people.

Preserve us from 'unique.'

Meaning One: Unique [actual meaning] – being the only one of its kind; unlike anything else.

Meaning Two: 'Unique [as used by travel writers] – a bit different, a bit unusual, or the sort of place they haven't experienced before but is, in fact, quite common elsewhere.

If there is any element of doubt regarding a place's difference or unusualness, it's apparently acceptable to refer to it as 'quite' or 'fairly' unique, notwithstanding Meaning One.

≈

Assuming we're not actually in a Saudi Arabian holy city, then it's probably safe to say that the writer thinks by saying somewhere is 'the Mecca of,' that this place is quite good for something or other. Surfing maybe. Or shopping.

Please note, this construction doesn't work with English holy places. "Head to the Lake District – the Canterbury of outdoor enthusiasts" just doesn't do the same job. The actual Mecca, on the other hand, is the Mecca of pilgrimages.

By the way, if we're not in the Mecca of something or other, we might instead be in an 'oasis' or a 'paradise.' They amount to the same thing.

≈

Writers spend weeks or months travelling around a place, but in the end they have to come up with an order of priorities – the things or places that, with limited time, we should see first or not miss. This is where the 'Don't miss,' 'Must see,' 'Top Ten' recommendations come in.

However, if we tried not to miss everything we shouldn't miss, saw everything we must see, and ticked off the entire Top Ten – well, frankly, there wouldn't be any time left to get off the beaten track and have a cocktail in a hostelry.

I think we should miss something now and again, just to keep travel writers on their toes.

You're in the local market. Look around you. Are there more than two other shoppers, besides you? According to the guidebook, that means it's officially 'vibrant.'

Has one shopper walked relatively quickly past another shopper? Congratulations, it is now 'bustling.'

Have you heard one stallholder talk to a shopper, perhaps to tell them the price of something? Bingo – this market is *so* 'buzzing.'

On the stall, is some of the fruit red and are some of the vegetables green? That makes it 'colourful,' which you'll have to agree is one hell of a market. Or possibly a description of your local Tesco.

Peru is 'the new' Albania. That's all they have to say to get our attention.

I don't know anything about either country, and I'm pretty sure that one doesn't relate to the other in any way whatsoever. But it's in a travel article and I'm thinking about it. Now I want to go to Peru. Job done.

I realise the battle is lost, and the ramparts well and truly stormed, but one more time, just for the record – attack ships on fire off the shoulder of Orion, and C-beams glittering in the dark near the Tannhauser gate, those are 'awesome' sights. As defined, they evoke a sense of awe, emotions that overwhelm in their intensity.

Our pizza, on the other hand, is not awesome.

Finally, a defence.

The reason so many travel writers use clichés is that it's very hard not to.

Clichés might be crimes against clear, inspiring writing, but they are very easy to use and they often sound so right. Just perfect for that hidden gem of a beach or village, spot-on for that awesome experience. Most travel writers don't even know they're doing it, because the words and phrases are so familiar – hell, they're clichés, being over-used is what they do for a living.

And believe me, I know – there's no point in going through any of my work and trying to catch me out. I am guilty as charged. My work is truly a collection of contrasts with something for everyone.

Obviously, it would be better for travel writers to use fewer clichés. They are defined as expressions that have become so over-used that they have lost their original meaning, even to the point of being annoying. And they

177

can be annoying, because most of them are just lazy, shorthand ways of describing places and things.

They let the travel writer off the hook, because they don't require any original thought. Using clichés makes the destinations or experiences themselves dull, blurred and homogenous – it's hard to know what's distinctive when you read about awesome waterfall after awesome meal after awesome hike.

Sadly, clichéd travel writing often gets a free pass, because readers are normally there not for the words but for the destination, the experience or the photographs. Good travel writing is a bonus, but it's definitely not a given.

For my part, I do my best to write well, and I want readers to be enthused by the things that I write. If, now and again, I guide you towards a hidden gem that's off the beaten track, then I hope you'll forgive me as you survey the verdant, panoramic view. You will? Awesome.

WHY YOU DON'T REALLY
NEED A GUIDEBOOK

IF YOU'VE EVER USED a travel guidebook, you'll know they can be useful, insightful, helpful and informative. I should know, I wrote dozens of editions of Rough Guides over the years, and I also travelled extensively around the world using every other brand of travel guide. I enjoyed writing them and I still like using them.

While guidebooks aren't the only way to find out information these days, there's something reassuring about that weighty paper object in your bag. It's never going to run out of power and, unlike a Kindle, if you drop it in the bath – wait, no, that will be terrible for it, don't drop the book in the bath.

We rely on a guidebook "to tell it like it is," or at least to help us out in our chosen destination. We take the book's word for it, we rely on the writer's recommendations and plan our itineraries according to their suggestions. Not just guidebooks, by the way. Blogs, posts, newspaper articles, travel magazines – we take it as read that the authors know what they are talking about. We value their opinions; we go to places on the strength of their knowledge and the breadth of their descriptions.

Oh boy, where to start.

If you've ever used a travel guidebook, you'll also know they can be infuriating, misleading, out of date and sometimes just plain wrong. The writers don't always get it right, even when they try their best; and sometimes the wrong bits are not their fault at all. Then again ... well, how about I show you how to rely on the most accurate parts of your travel guide and not worry about the rest of it?

Let's lift the lid a little, peer in, give the information a poke and see if we can trust it. Spoiler: you're not always going to be able to. Sometimes, you would be better off not buying a guidebook and simply giving the first person you encounter on the street £13.99 and asking them where the best restaurant in town is.

But we live in hope, so let's give whatever guide you have in your hand a chance.

First, check the publication date.

Just because it's on the bookshop shelf or in the Amazon basket doesn't mean it's up to date. Most guide-books are only updated every two to three years, some-times longer, and it will have been researched anything up to a year or more before publication. A guidebook with last year's date in it could easily contain information that's already two or three years old.

It doesn't mean that *everything* in the book is wrong or out of date – but you can at least count on prices having gone up, restaurants closing down or changing hands, and great new bars not even mentioned. Think of the things that have changed in your hometown in the last year or two, and then imagine holding a guidebook writer to account for not keeping up with places that didn't even exist when they visited.

By the way, guides with this year's date on and splashed with the words 'Updated annually' don't fill me full of confidence either. The research will still have been done up to a year ago, and ask yourself how in-depth an updating job the author can do in such a short time? One of the reasons most guidebooks only get updated every two or three years is because it takes a lot of time to cover an entire city or a country and do it properly.

Assuming you've got the most up-to-date version available, your guidebook is an invaluable planning tool. You can figure out roughly how much money you'll need, how you can get around and what you'd like to see. There are photos and descriptions; this is starting to get exciting. You're being inspired by what you read.

But planning only gets you so far. Don't bet your life on the guidebook being exactly right, especially about the nuts and bolts of travelling. Things change – and guide-book writers aren't infallible – so don't assume that every word is Gospel. The world is full of perplexed people standing outside closed and shuttered buildings, saying "But the *Rough Guide* said …"

If time and money are issues, and you simply must see that place or do that thing, then double-check the information – on travel forums, websites and social media.

At which point, you're wondering why you're bothering with a guidebook in the first place? If you have to confirm and cross-reference, then what's the point of the written word on the printed page? Factual authority and creative description, you might think are good answers, and they are decent reasons to stick with a book that might be a little out of date, practically speaking.

The writer's account of the Taj Mahal has fired your interest; it reads well and seems insightful and informative. It's better than the blog-post on 'Ten Great Things To Do in India,' which simply says "Awesome building." The essential facts won't have changed – I'm prepared to bet that the Taj Mahal was still commissioned in 1632 by the Mughal emperor Shah Jahan, and is still made of white marble, whatever date is on your guidebook. You have to look up the exact opening hours, so what? Score one to the guide.

We're going to give the book and the writer a break as far as the historical and cultural research is concerned. If they are good at their job, this is the easiest part – desk work, looking up facts, stitching them together in a coherent narrative, making it sound interesting. That's just writing, and even travel writers can do it, just as long as they don't copy it all off Wikipedia without double-checking sources and dates. Like, for example, the stuff I found out about the Taj Mahal, which might actually have been built in 1923 out of cream cheese, for all I know. The point is, I'll trust the travel writer to have done a proper job.

However – and you must have known this was coming – you are going to have to learn to read between the lines with the rest of the information in the book. And this is primarily because guidebook writers don't have the time or the money to visit, or stay and eat in, every place included in their guide. Bit of a shock? Sorry.

In the olden days, the Golden Age of guidebook writing – say, the 1980s and 1990s – publishers gave authors advances, and sometimes even free flights and expenses, and sent them off around the world to write travel books. The money was never *that* great, but it did at least allow you to spend a reasonable amount of time in a place and write a decent book. When the book started to sell, you got royalty payments each year, which helped fund further trips and meant that you got to know your destination even better. This way, I went to Barcelona, for example, over thirty times – and lived in places such as Sicily, Portugal and Hong Kong for up to six months at a time while researching the guides. They were good books, though I say it myself. Eventually, I'd been everywhere that I wrote about, because I had the time and money to do so.

It's different now. Advances, royalties, profit margins and publication schedules have shrunk – it's a tough business writing and selling guidebooks, when everything on the internet is free. Some destination and travel blogs are lovingly curated and amazingly detailed, and don't charge a penny for the information. You'd be mad not to use those, along with Tripadvisor and everything else, for spot-on, locally sourced reviews of hotels, restaurants and bars.

(By the way, let's not go overboard about Tripadvisor. If the top choice in a town is a takeaway burger bar – quite a common occurrence – and the hottest new restaurant is nowhere to be seen, you begin to doubt the validity of the reviews. But take a wider look. There's something reliable about the wisdom of crowds, and if the overall ratings for a particular place are high and the overall complaints low, then probably what you've got is a decent restaurant.)

Where does this all leave the poor old guidebook writer, with less time, a flying visit and an increasingly limited budget? Playing catch-up, is where, and doing the best they can, which is why you need to exercise a bit of due diligence as you're scanning the reviews and wondering where to spend your money.

There might be a couple of hundred hotel reviews in a lengthy guidebook, maybe more, so it's a tough job to have inspected them all, let alone actually slept in them. You couldn't do it on one trip, and you couldn't keep going back to them all to see if things had changed, even over several trips, which would be a few years apart in any case.

Consequently, if a guidebook review sounds a bit vague, and talks mostly about the hotel's location or price (both of which you can find out from its website), then chances are the writer hasn't actually visited it in person.

"Reasonably priced city-centre hotel, near the cathedral" doesn't tell you anything you can't figure out yourself from the map. In fact, I'd go further. If there's a generic review like that, also featuring a suspiciously specific fact ("Reasonably priced city-centre hotel with gold bath taps, near the cathedral,"), then I'll bet there's a photo of the gold-tapped room on the hotel website.

Conversely, if there's some heartfelt, personal detail in the review – plumpness of the bed, street noise in the night, fantastic water pressure, complimentary cake on arrival – then the writer probably experienced it first-hand. Unless they made it up to sound like they had really been, and they're just messing with you now. To be fair, you can usually tell. Read a dozen hotel reviews in any town in any guidebook and you'll be able to tell where the writer has stayed.

Whatever goes for hotels, goes double for cafés and restaurants. If a restaurant review gushes about dishes and recipes that (there's a surprise) are also picked out on the restaurant's own website, or if it only describes décor that you can see in the website images – well, go figure. Even if every single restaurant is lovingly and personally described, you also have to bear in mind that the guidebook reviews are just a snapshot of all the restaurants in that city. There's no way the writer had time to check out every restaurant on their brief visit. Maybe they missed the best place of all, especially if it was – cliché alert! – a hidden gem?

Also, ever notice how the same restaurants appear in every guidebook? That's because (whisper it gently) they copy each other – if a great-sounding restaurant is in one guide, you can bet the authors of a competing guide will want to check it out and include it too. That doesn't necessarily make it a bad restaurant, just because it's in several guidebooks. But look around you – do most of your fellow diners appear to be tourists? Really? How did that happen?

For the most part, guidebook writers aren't bad people. It's a job with limited time and money. They have to cut some corners to get the work done. If that means an occasional bodged-together review, that's not the worst thing in the world. After all, they probably have done some research, even if not on the ground. These places will also be in other guidebooks, or have been recommended in some other way, and if you stay or eat there you'll probably do just fine. (I realise that 'doing just fine' isn't a sufficient recommendation if you're about to blow significant sums on a top chef's garlanded restaurant and want to know if it's really worth it. But in that case, seriously, what are you expecting from my two-line review? Get a Michelin guide or track down a food writer's review – those guys really have eaten in all the restaurants.)

What I'm saying here is – cut the guidebook some slack. For all the reasons mentioned, it isn't going to be right every time. But you'll soon get a feel for whether or not – generally speaking – the guide can be trusted.

So, some of the prices are out of date? But did the writer get it spot on about the feel of the place or the experience? Was the hotel proprietor as charming as they said? Did the restaurant fulfil the promise in the book? If so, then you can trust that the writer did their job properly and let the minor changes go.

Once you trust the book to be mostly all right – I realise how damning with faint praise that sounds – you start to build up a relationship with the guide and possibly even with the writer. People love their guidebooks; they call them their 'Bibles;' they have a favourite series, which better have been the Rough Guides, is all I'm saying. As a guidebook writer, I felt I was speaking directly to readers with every suggestion or review, and they returned the favour. I used to get letters and emails full of praise all the time from satisfied travellers, which is not normal in most other spheres of working life.

Mind you, travellers and readers also seemed to be more forgiving than other consumers – or possibly the bar was set so low with some other guidebooks that Rough Guides got the benefit of the doubt. Either way, I also got numerous letters and emails that said things like, "The hotel you mentioned had closed down a year ago, the museum was derelict, the restaurant was awful, and we got robbed at knifepoint, but we found a great little bar up the road, *and thanks so much, the guide was brilliant.*"

One man used to write to me regularly about his trips to Spain – huge, handwritten screeds with recommendations of bars and restaurants that he suggested I should check out. They all sounded fantastic, just the sorts of places that I'd be interested in including in the guide. Unfortunately – as he confessed at the end of every lovingly detailed paragraph – because he'd been completely pissed, he couldn't remember the names of any of them, or the streets they were on, though one may have had a blue door or was it near the church?

And now, finally, as you've come to trust large parts of your guidebook – and perhaps have warmed to the writer, as their personality starts to shine through – it's time to put the book away. Because the truth is, you don't always need it to find your way around.

If you wander around City A, Country B or Continent C with your nose firmly in the *Lonely Rough Let's Go Time Out Frommer's Guide*, you will miss the entire point of your trip in the first place, which was to experience something new. By definition, if it's in the guidebook, it's not new. Someone has been there before, and possibly thousands of people are there now, bumping into each other because they have their noses in the same guidebook.

Go down a different street, eat in a restaurant not in the guide, ask a local, sleep under the stars – there are all sorts of ways you can wander down the road less travelled. I know that's probably why you wanted a guidebook in the first place – so that someone else had done the hard work, filtered the good from the bad, and helped you decide what was worth your time and money. But there's got to be space for trial and error – for your own discoveries – for adventure. That's the best kind of travel memory to take back home, that time you ate in a little place around the corner, in the back streets, which – you will proclaim proudly – "wasn't in the guidebook."

I'll let you into a secret. You don't need to be a travel writer to find a place like that. Just ask people. Hotel staff, tourist office employees, the police, delivery guys, even just strangers on the street – I'll talk to them all in the quest for a fantastic restaurant.

Here's the trick though. Because you look like a tourist – you do, really – they might tell you about the sort of place they think you should go, rather than the kind of place we're talking about. They may not imagine for one minute that you want to sit in their neighbourhood joint, in a brightly lit room with mismatched furniture, no menu and no one who speaks English. But you do, because the food will be great and even if it isn't, you'll have had a memorable experience.

You need to ask them, "Where do you eat with your family?" or "Where can I eat real Mexican/Portuguese/Thai food?" or even "Where can I go where there aren't any tourists where the food is great?" That's the message you want to get across. Can't understand the menu? Or even, no menu at all? Don't let it worry you – no one ever minds you pointing at dishes on other peoples' tables. Give a thumbs-up if you have to. The waiter will get the idea. I've been taken into the kitchen before now and shown what they have, with not a word of English being exchanged. Hence, I suspect, the dish of sautéed pangolin liver in a stag-beetle *jus*.

Just kidding, though I did get served grilled shark embryo once.

Incidentally, I've never fully subscribed to the 'If it's empty, the restaurant can't be any good' hypothesis. Perhaps you're just too early? Turn up to eat dinner in Spain at nine-thirty at night, for example, and they're just setting the tables. You will eat a great meal – often in splendid isolation – and then put your coat on to leave at eleven p.m. just as everyone else arrives for dinner.

I've eaten in restaurants where they had to wake the chef up; restaurants that were basically someone's lounge; restaurants in castles, monasteries, prisons and ships; restaurants in jungles, on beaches, up mountains and in gorges; restaurants where I had to choose my meal from fish tanks; and restaurants where no one – and I mean no one – had ever seen or spoken to a foreigner before.

By just wandering around and asking questions, I've also found museums that weren't supposed to be open; been on personally escorted tours around otherwise dodgy neighbourhoods; discovered that if I stayed another day I'd coincide with a special festival; and been to unadvertised gigs in Roman amphitheatres.

Every single experience was memorable. None was in a guidebook. Indeed, I never put everything I knew into my guidebooks, because some places were special to me, and you will be able to find your own special places too. In fact, I insist.

Just by staying in that city, travelling around that country, seeing that sight, eating that meal – at just that point – you are the most experienced, up-to-date authority there is. You've just paid to get in. You know exactly how much it cost. Or, whatever opening hours it stated in the guidebook, you just got there five minutes too late and will have to come back tomorrow. And you can keep this useful information to yourself, or you can share it. What else is Twitter, Facebook and Instagram but a big old collection of travel tips, boasts, blags, recommendations and reviews?

In the end, guidebooks can only get you so far. They can do a job but they can't do *all* the jobs. One-to-one, face-to-face advice and inspiration – that's the mother-lode for other travellers. That's the stuff people trust. Those are the things you want to hear about, from real people who have just been – not from someone sat at a desk, who was last there a year or two ago.

I know, given the career I've had and the books I've written, I shouldn't really say this, but:

You are the guidebook. Be the guidebook.

ALSO BY JULES BROWN

Born to Travel series

Don't Eat the Puffin

Never Pack an Ice-Axe

Watch Out for Pirates

Journeys

Not Cool: Europe by Train in a Heatwave

Guidebooks

Montenegro: A Trust-Me Travel Guide

DID YOU LIKE THIS BOOK?

Well of course, I hope you did! But as an author, there's no real way for me to tell if you enjoyed reading my book, unless you take a minute to leave a rating or a review on Amazon, Goodreads or Bookbub.

I know that's a bit of a pain if you've just finished a paperback book, but I thought I'd take a minute to explain what a huge difference it makes when kind readers such as yourself leave a rating or review.

Firstly, I get to hear directly how much you liked the book. It's a thrill when anyone buys my work, and I get another buzz when I hear how you felt about my writing and my travel experiences. Mostly, I just sit here, writing stories and sending them out into the world. It's great when they bounce back from a reader with some feedback, whatever that might be.

The other reason is that, of course, I'd like as many people as possible to read my books. Ratings and reviews really help with publicising my books to a wider audience. In fact, after buying and reading a book, the single best thing you can do to help an author whose work you like is to leave them a review.

So, many thanks in advance, and happy travels!

ABOUT THE AUTHOR

Jules Brown took his first solo trip around Europe when he was seventeen, and has been travelling and writing professionally since he published his first travel guide – to Scandinavia – in 1988.

Since then he has eaten a puffin in Iceland, got stuck up a mountain in the Lake District, crash-landed in Iran, fallen off a husky sled in Canada, and was stranded on a Mediterranean island. Not all of those things were his fault.

He wrote Rough Guide travel books for over thirty years, but now that he no longer has to copy down bus timetables for a living he doesn't know what to do with himself. So he comes up with ridiculous ideas for trips and then writes about them.

He still doesn't know what he wants to do when he grows up.

FIND OUT MORE

If you enjoyed this book, here's how to find out more about my upcoming books, projects, trips and events.

JOIN IN AT JULES TOLD ME!

I blog about travel and travel-writing at julestoldme.com, and I'd love to see you there! There are features on over thirty countries on the blog, plus posts about life as a travel writer and how to self-publish. Follow the blog and sign up for the newsletter and you'll be the first to learn about new posts, books and travels.

BOOKS BY TRUST-ME TRAVEL

Trust-Me Travel is the name of my book publishing company – you'll find it at trustmetravel.com. As well as travel memoirs and adventures, I write and publish travel guides with a twist.

Printed in Great Britain
by Amazon

84027706R00119